Savvy

GOD'S TRUTH FOR A LIFE THAT WORKS

PAM GILLASPIE
with JAN SILVIOUS

**Savvy: God's Truth for a Life That
Works**

Copyright © 2018 by Pam Gillaspie
Published by Precept Ministries
International
P.O. Box 182218
Chattanooga, Tennessee 37422
www.precept.org

ISBN 978-1-62119-715-7

Dedicated to . . .

Jan
Thank you for letting me walk with you.

Acknowledgements

My deep thanks to my Bible study friends who patiently walked through the pilot class with me and gave excellent feedback along the way. Your suggestion to include all of the text of Scripture in the lessons has made this workbook so much more user-friendly. Thank you, as always, to my family—Dave, Katie, Brad, Jackie, Mom and Dad—I love you all to the moon and back! Finally, thank you to my co-workers at Precept. Rick, Pete, and Paula; you're patient and make me look better than I am. I am grateful!

Savvy
GOD'S TRUTH FOR A LIFE THAT WORKS

Savvy

GOD'S TRUTH FOR A LIFE THAT WORKS

There is nothing quite like your favorite pair of jeans. You can dress them up, you can dress them down. You can work in them, play in them, shop in them . . . live in them. They always feel right. It is my hope that the structure of this Bible study will fit you like those jeans; that it will work with your life right now, right where you are whether you're new to this whole Bible thing or whether you've been studying the Book for years!

How is this even possible? Smoke and mirrors, perhaps? The new mercilessly thrown in the deep end? The experienced given pompoms and the job of simply cheering others on? None of the above.

Flexible inductive studies are designed with options that will allow you to go as deep each week as you desire. If you're just starting out and feeling a little over-whelmed, stick with the main text and don't think a second thought about the sidebar assignments. If you're looking for a challenge, then take the sidebar prompts and go ahead and dig all the way to China! As you move along through the study, think of the sidebars and "Digging Deeper" boxes as that 2% of Lycra that you find in certain jeans . . . the wiggle-room that will help them fit just right.

Beginners may find that they want to start adding in some of the optional assign-ments as they go along. Experts may find that when three children are throwing up for three days straight, foregoing those assignments for the week is the way to live wisely.

Life has a way of ebbing and flowing, and this study is designed to ebb and flow right along with it!

Enjoy!

Contents

Savvy
GOD'S TRUTH FOR A LIFE THAT WORKS

How to use this study

Flexible inductive studies meet you where you are and take you as far as you want to go.

1. **WEEKLY STUDY:** The main text guides you through the complete topic of study for the week.

2. **FYI:** For Your Information boxes provide bite-sized material to shed additional light on the topic.

3. **ONE STEP FURTHER and other sidebar info:** Sidebars give you the option to push yourself a little further. If you have extra time or are looking for an extra challenge, you can try one, all, or any number in between! These sidebars give you the ultimate in flexibility.

4. **DIGGING DEEPER boxes:** If you're looking to go further, Digging Deeper sections will help you sharpen your skills as you continue to mine the truths of Scripture for yourself.

Lesson One

Where Are You Building?

"Therefore everyone who hears these words of Mine and acts on them, may be compared to a wise man who built his house on the rock. And the rain fell, and the floods came, and the winds blew and slammed against that house; and yet it did not fall, for it had been founded on the rock."
–Jesus, Matthew 7:24-25

The world we're living in is changing. Rapidly. Make no mistake. Strategies that worked for our parents don't work today because our world is fundamentally different. Recently, I met a woman who grew up in Michigan and then spent 20 years doing missionary work in Holland. Her comment on moving back to the United States and settling in New England: "It is surprisingly similar to Holland." It wasn't a compliment. She returned home to a *different* country. The United States she left after college no longer exists.

If you live somewhere else in the world, your home has changed, too. Technology has connected us to information and to one another in ways that only science fiction writers dream of. But for every uplifting "GoFundMe" story, there is a tale from the dark side of technology, the anonymity cloak that both hides sin and fuels vices.

Still, no matter how dark the world becomes, truth remains. As we walk through the pages of Scripture in this study which will focus heavily on the book of Proverbs, we will begin to see for ourselves God's timeless truths and discern how to apply them in our ever-changing times! Our ancestors faced different battles, different trials, different wars. As they learned to *apply* God's timeless truths in their day, so we must learn how to apply them *today*. We must live wisely *today*, in *this* generation . . . we need to be savvy!

A THOUGHT FROM: *Pam*

Notes from Jan and me
In addition to sidebars that offer extra study options, you'll find sprinkled throughout the workbook notes from both Jan Silvious and me on applying Proverbs to life. Since Jan has been a mentor to me for years and is one of the wisest people I know, I couldn't resist asking her to drop in some gems of practical wisdom throughout this book! I am one of many who have been blessed to grow a little wiser by being able to walk with the wise. I know you'll be encouraged by Jan's gracious, yet straight-to-the-heart wisdom.

FYI:

If You're in a Class
Complete **Week One** together on your first day of class. This will be a great way to start getting to know one another and will help those who are newer to Bible study get their bearings.

Savvy
GOD'S TRUTH FOR A LIFE THAT WORKS

FYI:

Where do you need wisdom?

Take some time to consider where you need wisdom for the situations you face. Jot them down below. This will help you as you seek not only to know truth but also to apply it. I hope that you're coming to this study expectantly, looking for God's answers to your questions, because He gives wisdom to those who ask.

PRESUPPOSITIONS: WHAT ARE YOU BRINGING ALONG?

How do you define "wisdom"? What do you think makes a person or behavior "wise"?

How does secular culture define wise living? Do morals and ethics come into play or not? Explain.

If you disagree with the cultural definition(s), what struggle does this pose in your day-to-day life?

INDUCTIVE STUDY: LETTING GOD'S WORD SPEAK FOR ITSELF

While it's important to consider current views as we study, we want to do this to hold them up to the plumb line of God's perfect Word. We'll do this through a process called Inductive Bible Study which simply means that we'll be using the Bible as our primary resource.

This may sound simple and obvious, but an epidemic of biblical illiteracy is making this less and less common even in the Church as people increasingly follow the views of other people rather than taking time to discover God's truth for themselves.

There are three basic components to Inductive Bible Study: observation, interpretation, and application.

OBSERVATION

As we **OBSERVE** the text of Scripture, we read carefully and seek to answer the question: *What does the text say?* Slow and thoughtful reading is the core competency in observation and certain tools can help us do this.

- Asking 5 W and H questions – Who? What? When? Where? Why? and How?

- Identifying and marking **key words** – Key words are critical to understanding and typically repeated. When marking key words, you'll want to mark synonyms and pronouns too.

- Making **Lists** – Key words are a basis for lists. After we identify a key word, listing everything we learn about it helps us to better grasp what the text says.

If you're new to inductive study, relax! The study will lead you through the basic components and prompt you with questions along the way.

INTERPRETATION

Careful observation is invaluable for interpreting the text and answering the question: *What does the text mean?* As we interpret, we're looking for one meaning. It's not uncommon for people to mix up interpretation and application. You've probably witnessed this when you've heard a person ask, "What does this verse mean *to you?*"

The text of Scripture does not change meaning based on who is reading it. It means what its author intended. As an author, I have a purpose in writing. You may think I'm trying to say something other than what I said, but that does not change my meaning. It means either you misinterpreted or I didn't express myself clearly. Now the Word tells us that God speaks clearly but it's still possible for "the untaught and unstable" to "distort . . . the Scriptures, to their own destruction" (2 Peter 3:16).

When we interpret, we **OBSERVE** the text closely and then look for the one meaning God intended. Here are some tools that will help immensely in discovering the text's meaning:

- Paying close attention to **context** – The context is simply the setting in which something dwells.

- Checking **cross-references** – Cross-references are other places in Scripture that talk about the same topic.

- Allowing **Scripture to interpret Scripture** – The best commentary on Scripture is other Scripture. When we use cross-references we are allowing Scripture to interpret Scripture.

APPLICATION

Once we discover the meaning of the text, we can begin to apply it in our lives. Application needs to be anchored in the meaning of the text, but many and varied applications can come from one meaning. James, for example, talks about controlling the tongue in the third chapter of his letter. How that specifically applies day-to-day will probably be different in my life than yours, but it will be anchored in the same truth of honoring God through what we do and don't do. Bible study is never complete without application . . . and application starts at home. (And by "at home" I don't mean you apply the Word to your spouse and kids and then go after the neighbors! Application starts with *me!*)

The Goal: TRANSFORMATION!

If you're just the Bible rock star who can clobber all your friends with superior knowledge, there's a big problem. The goal of inductive study is never knowledge for knowledge's sake, but rather understanding of God's Word for transforming lives.

Putting on the Brakes

If the inductive "tools" seem overwhelming, just remember this: slow down. Good observation doesn't require colored pencils or a rigid process. Good observation happens when we slow down long enough to see what is obvious in the text. For some of us, slowing down can seem inefficient, but the truth is: good observation takes time.

FRAMING OUR STUDY

Since there are so many different views on wisdom in our world—from "just a cerebral activity" to "the end justifies the means"—we're going to see what Jesus says about wise and foolish living as we get started.

Our text comes from the end of His teaching on the Sermon on the Mount (found in Matthew 5–7) where Jesus tells His listeners the key difference between the wise and foolish man.

Observe the TEXT of SCRIPTURE:

READ Matthew 7:24-27 and **MARK** the phrases *wise man* and *foolish man*.

Matthew 7:24-27

24 "Therefore everyone who hears these words of Mine and acts on them, may be compared to a wise man who built his house on the rock.

25 "And the rain fell, and the floods came, and the winds blew and slammed against that house; and *yet* it did not fall, for it had been founded on the rock.

26 "Everyone who hears these words of Mine and does not act on them, will be like a foolish man who built his house on the sand.

27 "The rain fell, and the floods came, and the winds blew and slammed against that house; and it fell—and great was its fall."

Discuss with your GROUP or PONDER on your own . . .

Read Matthew 5:1-2 to help set this passage in context. What do these verses tell us about who is teaching, who is being taught, and where they are?

Considering Matthew 5:1-2, what is the "Therefore" in Matthew 7:24 there for?

Start with Prayer

You've probably heard it before and if we study together again, you'll hear it again. Whenever you read or study God's Word, first ask His Spirit to be your Guide. Jesus says that the Spirit will lead us into all truth.

Do I have to mark the text?

Nope. If you've ever been told that you *have to* mark the text to be a good Bible student, you may be understandably resistant. Still, marking key words can be helpful. When we mark, we identify words that repeat and are, therefore, important to the meaning. You don't *have to* mark the text, but likely if you try it, you'll see the benefit.

UNDERLINE in the text and list below the circumstances that came into the lives of both the wise and foolish men.

Did both men receive the same information? Was one disadvantaged in any way? What is the only difference?

Can you think of an example in your life when you *knew* the truth but did not *do* it? What resulted?

What about a good example? Can you think of a time when you *knew* what to do and *did* it?

Certainly "the rock" the wise man built his house on incorporates all the righteous acts Jesus includes in His sermon on the mount but not exclusively: righteousness is defined in every book of the Bible. As we will see in this study, the importance of knowing and acting on God's revealed Word is taught both implicitly and explicitly throughout the pages of Scripture. Wisdom is not simply hearing and understanding intellectually. Living wisely involves acting appropriately based on God's revealed truth; it is aligning our lives with God's wisdom.

As we progress through our study, we'll be looking at several proverbs each week that will define specific components of wisdom. We'll also be looking at other parts of Scripture to help us see the many facets of wisdom.

ONE STEP FURTHER:

Read the Sermon on the Mount

If you have some time this week, read or listen to all of Matthew 5–7. My pastor used to describe the Sermon on the Mount as "Jesus' words for Jesus' people!" Jot down below what you observed and learned.

Savvy

GOD'S TRUTH FOR A LIFE THAT WORKS

THE WISE DO:

List It

Let's start a running list of what wisdom does and how it benefits those who find it. You can continue to add to this as we work our way through Proverbs. Depending on how detailed you are, you may want to use a separate notebook.

Observe PROVERBS 1

READ Proverbs 1 and **MARK** every occurrence of the repeated word *wisdom* (include the synonym *understanding* and any others you notice.)

Proverbs 1

1 The proverbs of Solomon the son of David, king of Israel:

2 To know wisdom and instruction,

To discern the sayings of understanding,

3 To receive instruction in wise behavior,

Righteousness, justice and equity;

4 To give prudence to the naive,

To the youth knowledge and discretion,

5 A wise man will hear and increase in learning,

And a man of understanding will acquire wise counsel,

6 To understand a proverb and a figure,

The words of the wise and their riddles.

7 The fear of the LORD is the beginning of knowledge;

Fools despise wisdom and instruction.

8 Hear, my son, your father's instruction

And do not forsake your mother's teaching;

9 Indeed, they are a graceful wreath to your head

And ornaments about your neck.

10 My son, if sinners entice you,

Do not consent.

11 If they say, "Come with us,

Let us lie in wait for blood,

Let us ambush the innocent without cause;

12 Let us swallow them alive like Sheol,

Even whole, as those who go down to the pit;

13 We will find all *kinds* of precious wealth,

We will fill our houses with spoil;

14 Throw in your lot with us,

We shall all have one purse,"

15 My son, do not walk in the way with them.

Keep your feet from their path,

16 For their feet run to evil

And they hasten to shed blood.

17 Indeed, it is useless to spread the *baited* net

In the sight of any bird;

18 But they lie in wait for their own blood;

They ambush their own lives.

19 So are the ways of everyone who gains by violence;

It takes away the life of its possessors.

20 Wisdom shouts in the street,

She lifts her voice in the square;

21 At the head of the noisy *streets* she cries out;

At the entrance of the gates in the city she utters her sayings:

22 "How long, O naive ones, will you love being simple-minded?

And scoffers delight themselves in scoffing

And fools hate knowledge?

23 "Turn to my reproof,

Behold, I will pour out my spirit on you;

I will make my words known to you.

24 "Because I called and you refused,

I stretched out my hand and no one paid attention;

25 And you neglected all my counsel

And did not want my reproof;

26 I will also laugh at your calamity;

I will mock when your dread comes,

27 When your dread comes like a storm

And your calamity comes like a whirlwind,

When distress and anguish come upon you.

28 "Then they will call on me, but I will not answer;

They will seek me diligently but they will not find me,

29 Because they hated knowledge

And did not choose the fear of the LORD.

30 "They would not accept my counsel,

They spurned all my reproof.

31 "So they shall eat of the fruit of their own way

And be satiated with their own devices.

32 "For the waywardness of the naive will kill them,

And the complacency of fools will destroy them.

33 "But he who listens to me shall live securely

And will be at ease from the dread of evil."

THE WISE DON'T/ THE FOOLISH DO:

List It

Let's also start a running list of what wisdom doesn't do (which often corresponds precisely with what the foolish do).

Discuss with your GROUP or PONDER on your own . . .

Besides wisdom, what other key words or concepts did you notice?

What were your general observations on the text?

What questions do you want answered as we study?

A THOUGHT FROM:

Making Up for Lost Time

For years I have slogged through the book of Proverbs in the process of reading through the Bible. The problem has not been with the Word of God but with my attitude toward the man God used to give us the book—Solomon.

I largely "missed out" on the depth of Proverbs for years because of my attitude. My prayer is that you won't make my mistake!

Isn't it amazing that God uses flawed people like you and me to accomplish His purposes? God used Solomon, whose heart turned away from the Lord, to give us Proverbs. We should never doubt the truth Paul tells us in 2 Timothy 3:16 that all Scripture is inspired by God and profitable for teaching, reproof, correction, and training in righteousness.

Right now, I'm making up for lost time in Proverbs! I sure hope you're enjoying the depth of wisdom in this book as much as I am!

a Closer Look

READ Proverbs 1:1-7 again and **MARK** every occurrence of the repeated word *instruction.* (Include any synonyms you notice.)

Proverbs 1:1-7

1   The proverbs of Solomon the son of David, king of Israel:

2   To know wisdom and instruction,
    To discern the sayings of understanding,

3   To receive instruction in wise behavior,
    Righteousness, justice and equity;

4   To give prudence to the naive,
    To the youth knowledge and discretion,

5   A wise man will hear and increase in learning,
    And a man of understanding will acquire wise counsel,

6   To understand a proverb and a figure,
    The words of the wise and their riddles.

7   The fear of the LORD is the beginning of knowledge;
    Fools despise wisdom and instruction.

Discuss with your GROUP or PONDER on your own . . .

According to verse 1:1, who wrote these proverbs? What was his position? Who was his famous father?

What is the purpose of the proverbs? What does it involve?

How can proverbs benefit the naive and the young?

GOD'S TRUTH FOR A LIFE THAT WORKS

How will they benefit those who are already wise?

How does the fool differ from the young or naive?

What category do you think you fall in today—wise, young, or naive? Why?

Read Proverbs 1:8-19 again and **MARK** every occurrence of the repeated word *instruction* (include any synonyms you notice). Also **MARK** *sinners* and pronouns referring to them.

Proverbs 1:8-19

8 Hear, my son, your father's instruction
   And do not forsake your mother's teaching;

9 Indeed, they are a graceful wreath to your head
   And ornaments about your neck.

10 My son, if sinners entice you,
   Do not consent.

11 If they say, "Come with us,
   Let us lie in wait for blood,
   Let us ambush the innocent without cause;

12 Let us swallow them alive like Sheol,
   Even whole, as those who go down to the pit;

13 We will find all *kinds* of precious wealth,
   We will fill our houses with spoil;

14 Throw in your lot with us,
   We shall all have one purse,"

15 My son, do not walk in the way with them.
   Keep your feet from their path,

16 For their feet run to evil
   And they hasten to shed blood.

FYI:

Repetitions and Contrasts
Repeated words and phrases in the text help us identify main ideas and themes. At times they help us see major contrasts also. Did you notice that Solomon writes to help people "know wisdom and instruction" (v. 2) but that fools "despise wisdom and instruction" (v. 7)? We'll continue to see this major contrast throughout the book.

ONE STEP FURTHER:

David and Solomon
If you have time this week, explore the lives of David and Solomon. Take this opportunity to use a concordance to search out where their accounts are in the Bible and then read up on them as much as you like. Record what you discover below.

Savvy
GOD'S TRUTH FOR A LIFE THAT WORKS

17   Indeed, it is useless to spread the *baited* net
     In the sight of any bird;

18   But they lie in wait for their own blood;
     They ambush their own lives.

19   So are the ways of everyone who gains by violence;
     It takes away the life of its possessors.

Discuss with your GROUP or PONDER on your own . . .

Whose teaching does Solomon appeal to in verses 8 and 9? What is it compared to?

How does this compare with instruction you have given or received?

What do verses 8-19 warn against in general?

Mark both instances of "do not" in this section. What specific warnings did you see? How do they differ?

What kinds of invitations to evil do you deal with today? What kinds call to those who are older? Younger?

Come with us!

Never underestimate the human desire to "belong." It's easy to read Proverbs 1 and think, "I would never . . ." or "My kids would never . . . ." Still, don't miss the perverted call to belonging, the perversion of unity that enticing sinners offer (boldface is for emphasis):

• Come with **us** . . .

• Let **us** lie in wait . . .

• Let **us** ambush . . .

• Let **us** swallow . . .

• **We** will find . . .

• **We** will fill . . .

• Throw in your lot with **us** . . .

• **We** shall all have **one** purse . . .

"Trust me!"

Isn't it interesting that the sinners who entice and invite others to join in harming the innocent and stealing, also say, "We shall all have one purse"? How do you decide who to trust? Do you think it is wise to trust someone who has shown himself untrustworthy?

What drives sinners? What do they want to gain and how?

What will their behavior reap in the end?

How can we avoid their trap? Answer from the text.

Read Proverbs 1:20-33 again and **MARK** *reproof*. Next **MARK** *naive one, scoffers, fools,* and pronouns referring to them. Finally, **UNDERLINE** what these people do or neglect to do.

Proverbs 1:20-33

20 Wisdom shouts in the street,

   She lifts her voice in the square;

21 At the head of the noisy *streets* she cries out;

   At the entrance of the gates in the city she utters her sayings:

22 "How long, O naive ones, will you love being simple-minded?

   And scoffers delight themselves in scoffing

   And fools hate knowledge?

23 "Turn to my reproof,

   Behold, I will pour out my spirit on you;

   I will make my words known to you.

24 "Because I called and you refused,

   I stretched out my hand and no one paid attention;

25 And you neglected all my counsel

   And did not want my reproof;

26 I will also laugh at your calamity;

   I will mock when your dread comes,

27 When your dread comes like a storm

ONE STEP FURTHER:

Word Studies:
Three Hebrew words that appear throughout Proverbs are worth exploring further! If you have time this week, investigate these repeating words and record what you learn.

Wise: *chakam*

Wise: *sakal*

Wisdom: *chokmah*

Discern/Understand (verb): *biyn*

Understanding (noun): *biynah*

Savvy

GOD'S TRUTH FOR A LIFE THAT WORKS

ONE STEP FURTHER:

Word Study: Reproof

If you have time this week, find the Hebrew word translated "reproof" and see how it is used in Proverbs and the rest of the Old Testament. Record your findings below. Then, consider how you respond to reproof!

And your calamity comes like a whirlwind,

When distress and anguish come upon you.

28 "Then they will call on me, but I will not answer;

They will seek me diligently but they will not find me,

29 Because they hated knowledge

And did not choose the fear of the LORD.

30 "They would not accept my counsel,

They spurned all my reproof.

31 "So they shall eat of the fruit of their own way

And be satiated with their own devices.

32 "For the waywardness of the naive will kill them,

And the complacency of fools will destroy them.

33 "But he who listens to me shall live securely

And will be at ease from the dread of evil."

Discuss with your GROUP or PONDER on your own . . .

How is wisdom personified in verses 20-33?

What questions does she call out and to whom? How is each group described?

What does she offer? How and *how often* does she offer? What response does she seek?

How do you typically respond to counsel? What about to reproof?

How will wisdom treat those who refuse her? How thoroughly is the rejection of wisdom described? (Look back at your underlined phrases to answer this.)

When do foolish people search for wisdom? Why do you think they wait?

What will those who refuse wisdom eventually reap?

We live in a world where people love their own evil (John 3:19) but dread everyone else's (Proverbs 1:33). According to Proverbs 1:33, what is the solution to both? Are you living in this truth?

@THE END OF THE DAY . . .

Take a few minutes to think and pray though what you've learned this week. Then summarize the key points below. Before you finish, write a one-sentence summary describing Proverbs 1 (try to be concise and keep it to 140 characters or less!) and give it a simple hashtag.

Proverbs 1

One-Sentence Summary

A THOUGHT FROM:

There is a God . . .

As a Life Coach, I've spent a lot of time listening to people who want to move from "where they are to where they want to be."

In the process, I have found that the people who make it to "where they want to be" are always the people who know they can't get there on their own wisdom. They recognize their limitations. That's a great step forward for the wise. Proverbs 28:26 says it well: "He who trusts in his own heart is a fool...." One of my favorite refrigerator magnets says it this way: "There is a God and you are not Him." Drop the mic!

Sammy

GOD'S TRUTH FOR A LIFE THAT WORKS

HOW TO DO AN ONLINE WORD STUDY

For use with www.blueletterbible.org

1. Type in a Bible verse. Change the version to NASB. Click the "Search" button.

2. When you arrive at the next screen, you will see a button labeled "Tools" to the left of your verse.

   Hover over the "Tool" button and a list will pop up.

   Click the first button on the pop-up list—"Interlinear"—to take you to the concordance link.

3. Click on the Strong's number which is the link to the original word in Greek or Hebrew.

Clicking this number will bring up another screen that will give you a brief definition of the word as well as list every occurrence of the Greek word in the New Testament or Hebrew word in the Old Testament. Before running to a dictionary definition, scan places where it's used in Scripture and examine the general contexts.

Lesson Two
Lean In, Acquire Wisdom, Don't Let Go!

For the LORD gives wisdom;
From His mouth come knowledge and understanding.
–Proverbs 2:6

Wisdom comes from the "only wise God, through Jesus Christ" (*mono sopho theo dia Iesou Christou:* Romans 16:27) who is "the wisdom of God" (*Theou sophian:* 1 Corinthians 1:24). Proverbs exhorts us to lean in, to acquire it, and when we've found it, to hold on to it for dear life! In a broken world teeming with threats both real and imagined, those who keep sound wisdom walk stably and sleep sweetly.

ONE STEP FURTHER:

Proverbs 1–7

If you have time this week, go ahead and read all of Proverbs 1–7 together. It will give you more context to look at chapters 2–4 and get you prepared for upcoming lessons. As you read, note briefly the overall content of this section of Proverbs.

Observe the TEXT of PROVERBS 1–4

READ or **LISTEN** to Proverbs 1–4 (yes, the chapters, and yes, I know we looked at Proverbs 1 last week). The text for Proverbs 2–4 is included in this week's lesson, but you may choose to read in your Bible. Once you've read or listened to the text, respond to the questions below.

Discuss with your GROUP or PONDER on your own . . .

What address introduces each chapter in Proverbs 2–4 (5–7, too) and is sprinkled throughout the first seven chapters of the book? (This is a great phrase to mark!). What tone does it set?

What other repeating words or phrases did you notice, if any?

What questions would you like answered now that you have read these chapters?

What was the biggest thing that stuck out to you on your first read-through?

Observe PROVERBS 2

READ Proverbs 2 and **MARK** the *wise* word group (*wisdom, understanding, discernment, knowledge*, etc.) and the *evil* word group (*evil, darkness, devious, wicked*, etc.) distinctively. Be sure to include other synonyms and pronouns as appropriate.

Proverbs 2

1 My son, if you will receive my words

And treasure my commandments within you,

2 Make your ear attentive to wisdom,

Incline your heart to understanding;

3 For if you cry for discernment,
Lift your voice for understanding;

4 If you seek her as silver

And search for her as for hidden treasures;

5 Then you will discern the fear of the LORD

And discover the knowledge of God.

6 For the LORD gives wisdom;

From His mouth *come* knowledge and understanding.

7 He stores up sound wisdom for the upright;

He is a shield to those who walk in integrity,

8 Guarding the paths of justice,

And He preserves the way of His godly ones.

9 Then you will discern righteousness and justice

And equity *and* every good course.

10 For wisdom will enter your heart

And knowledge will be pleasant to your soul;

11 Discretion will guard you,

Understanding will watch over you,

12 To deliver you from the way of evil,

From the man who speaks perverse things;

13 From those who leave the paths of uprightness

To walk in the ways of darkness;

14 Who delight in doing evil

And rejoice in the perversity of evil;

15 Whose paths are crooked,

And who are devious in their ways;

16 To deliver you from the strange woman,

From the adulteress who flatters with her words;

17 That leaves the companion of her youth

And forgets the covenant of her God;

18 For her house sinks down to death

And her tracks *lead* to the dead;

19 None who go to her return again,

Nor do they reach the paths of life.

20 So you will walk in the way of good men

And keep to the paths of the righteous.

21 For the upright will live in the land

And the blameless will remain in it;

22 But the wicked will be cut off from the land

And the treacherous will be uprooted from it.

FYI:

Try Marking Your Bible!
Once you get the hang of marking, go ahead and try it in your Bible . . . unless that gives you hives. If it gives you hives, by all means, don't do it.

INDUCTIVE PRINCIPLES:

Bottom Line on Observation
Fundamentally, the way we observe the text well is to s...l...o...w d...o...w...n!

You don't have to use colored pencils, although they can be helpful; you don't need to follow set patterns of questions or bulleted lists, but you do need to s...l...o...w d...o...w...n enough to pay close attention!

Savvy
GOD'S TRUTH FOR A LIFE THAT WORKS

ONE STEP FURTHER:

Wise Guys (and Girls!)
Consider your own life for a bit. Who do you know personally that you consider "wise"? Write down their names, and then below each, write down the proverbs traits you have seen them display.

#1
Traits/Verse(s):

#2
Traits/Verse(s):

#3
Traits/Verse(s):

FYI:

Need Wisdom?
But if any of you lacks wisdom, let him ask of God, who gives to all generously and without reproach, and it will be given to him. But he must ask in faith without any doubting, for the one who doubts is like the surf of the sea, driven and tossed by the wind.
—James 1:5-6

Savvy
GOD'S TRUTH FOR A LIFE THAT WORKS

Discuss with your GROUP or PONDER on your own . . .

How does the first half of Proverbs 2 differ from the second?

What did you learn by **marking** the *wisdom* word group? Look back at your markings and make a simple list. You can divide the list by the specific words or group them together. Be sure to include verse references.

Summarize what Proverbs 2 teaches about wisdom and wise people.

How about the *evil* word group? Again, note where you **marked** and make a simple list of what you learned.

What is the fundamental difference between the wise and the wicked?

Did you notice the conditional statements in the first few verses of the chapter? *If* you did, *then* mark them in the text that follows and write them down. *If* you didn't, *then* look again. You should see them now.

a Closer Look

READ Proverbs 2:1-6 again and **MARK** the *if/then* statement. Be careful, the *if* portion is more robust. Then **UNDERLINE** the words associated with the *"if's"* (in case this is unclear, the first two are *receive* and *treasure*).

Proverbs 2:1-6

1 My son, if you will receive my words

   And treasure my commandments within you,

2 Make your ear attentive to wisdom,

   Incline your heart to understanding;

3 For if you cry for discernment,

   Lift your voice for understanding;

4 If you seek her as silver

   And search for her as for hidden treasures;

5 Then you will discern the fear of the LORD

   And discover the knowledge of God.

6 For the LORD gives wisdom;

   From His mouth *come* knowledge and understanding.

Discuss with your GROUP or PONDER on your own . . .

What must the son do to "discern the fear of the LORD and discover the knowledge of God"?

How does this compare with Proverbs 1:7?

Can anyone get wisdom on his own? Why/why not? Where does Proverbs 2:6 say it comes from?

INDUCTIVE PRINCIPLES:

Contrasts, Comparisons, Conditions, and Conclusions

Observing the text well involves paying attention to textual elements that help us understand how various words function together. *If/then* statements help us see conditional relationships between phrases while *terms of conclusion* like *so* and *therefore* cue us to look back in the text for something related.

Proverbs is full of *comparisons*, specifically *contrasts* that point out the radical and practical differences between wise and foolish living.

Savvy

FYI:

Equal Opportunity Evil

Evil is an equal opportunity employer. In the way of evil goes "the man who speaks perverse things" and "the strange woman . . . who flatters with her words." Different words—one *obviously* perverse, the other *covertly*—but both wholly evil.

While wisdom comes from God alone, what are ways we can do our part (so to speak) by receiving, treasuring, inclining? How do you "lean in"? How can you improve?

Where is your heart most inclined today? Is it toward God and His ways or does it gravitate toward other things? As you answer, consider where you spend your time and money. Also consider anything you tend to worry about.

According to verses 7-9, what characterizes a wise life? What other words are associated with it?

Besides the gift of wisdom itself, what tangible benefits come with wisdom?

Who populates "the way of evil"? What do these people do (always watch the verbs!)? What do they say? What delights them?

In what situation(s) do you (or yours) need either deliverance or guarding from evil today?

Based on Proverbs 2, where does the crooked path lead? Have you ever witnessed this firsthand?

Observe PROVERBS 3

READ Proverbs 3 and **MARK** the *wise* word group (*wisdom, understanding, discernment, knowledge,* etc.) Also **MARK** the phrase *"do not"* as well as any similar phrases you notice (for example *"let them not,"* etc.).

Proverbs 3

1 My son, do not forget my teaching,

But let your heart keep my commandments;

2 For length of days and years of life

And peace they will add to you.

3 Do not let kindness and truth leave you;

Bind them around your neck,
Write them on the tablet of your heart.

4 So you will find favor and good repute

In the sight of God and man.

5 Trust in the LORD with all your heart

And do not lean on your own understanding.

6 In all your ways acknowledge Him,

And He will make your paths straight.

7 Do not be wise in your own eyes;

Fear the LORD and turn away from evil.

8 It will be healing to your body

And refreshment to your bones.

9 Honor the LORD from your wealth

And from the first of all your produce;

Savvy
GOD'S TRUTH FOR A LIFE THAT WORKS

10 So your barns will be filled with plenty
And your vats will overflow with new wine.

11 My son, do not reject the discipline of the LORD
Or loathe His reproof,

12 For whom the LORD loves He reproves,
Even as a father *corrects* the son in whom he delights.

13 How blessed is the man who finds wisdom
And the man who gains understanding.

14 For her profit is better than the profit of silver
And her gain better than fine gold.

15 She is more precious than jewels;
And nothing you desire compares with her.

16 Long life is in her right hand;
In her left hand are riches and honor.

17 Her ways are pleasant ways
And all her paths are peace.

18 She is a tree of life to those who take hold of her,
And happy are all who hold her fast.

19 The LORD by wisdom founded the earth,
By understanding He established the heavens.

20 By His knowledge the deeps were broken up
And the skies drip with dew.

21 My son, let them not vanish from your sight;
Keep sound wisdom and discretion,

22 So they will be life to your soul
And adornment to your neck.

23 Then you will walk in your way securely
And your foot will not stumble.

24 When you lie down, you will not be afraid;
When you lie down, your sleep will be sweet.

25 Do not be afraid of sudden fear
Nor of the onslaught of the wicked when it comes;

26 For the LORD will be your confidence
And will keep your foot from being caught.

27 Do not withhold good from those to whom it is due,
When it is in your power to do *it.*

28 Do not say to your neighbor, "Go, and come back,
And tomorrow I will give *it,*" When you have it with you.

29 Do not devise harm against your neighbor,
While he lives securely beside you.

30 Do not contend with a man without cause,
If he has done you no harm.

31 Do not envy a man of violence
And do not choose any of his ways.

32 For the devious are an abomination to the LORD;
But He is intimate with the upright.

33 The curse of the LORD is on the house of the wicked,
But He blesses the dwelling of the righteous.

34 Though He scoffs at the scoffers,
Yet He gives grace to the afflicted.

35 The wise will inherit honor,
But fools display dishonor.

Discuss with your GROUP or PONDER on your own . . .

What teaching and commands are referred to in Proverbs 3:1? Where did they come from? What made them powerful, authoritative, and worth passing on?

What specific benefits do they bring?

What did you learn by **marking** the *wisdom* word group? Look back and make a simple list. You can divide the list by the specific words or look at them as a whole. Be sure to include the verse references.

Summarize what Proverbs 3 teaches about wisdom and wise people.

Consider your life for a moment. How are you walking in the way of wisdom? In what areas of life is walking wisely a challenge?

ONE STEP FURTHER:

What are the Teachings?
What teachings would a good Jewish father pass along to his sons? Check out Deuteronomy 6 and see for yourself! Record your findings below. Then hold up your life to the plumb line and see how you are doing with this command. Are you doing well? Where can you improve?

Savvy
GOD'S TRUTH FOR A LIFE THAT WORKS

A THOUGHT FROM: *Pam*

ScriptureTyper.com

One of my favorite tools for memorizing is an app called ScriptureTyper. Not only does it help you memorize, it helps you review, too! Try it out for yourself online at scripturetyper.com.

Digging Deeper

Hiding God's Word in Our Hearts

The Psalmist writes in Psalm 119:11, "Your word I have treasured in my heart, that I may not sin against You." Write down a proverb from each of the first four chapters to begin to commit to memory.

Proverbs 1:

Proverbs 2:

Proverbs 3:

Proverbs 4:

FYI:

The Potholes

In Proverbs 3, Solomon warns against some common-life potholes that don't seem terrible on the surface but can cause ruin. Both devising harm against your neighbor and picking a fight for no reason sound dark by almost any measuring stick, but leaning on one's own understanding? Hey, that danger almost sounds resourceful! Solomon warns against not only the big sins but also the subtle ones that sneak up on those who are unaware.

a Closer Look

READ Proverbs 3:1-12, 21-22 again and **MARK** references to *teaching* and *commandments* including synonyms and pronouns. Then **MARK** every reference to the *LORD*, again including synonyms and pronouns.

Proverbs 3:1-12, 21-22

1   My son, do not forget my teaching,

    But let your heart keep my commandments;

2   For length of days and years of life

    And peace they will add to you.

3   Do not let kindness and truth leave you;

    Bind them around your neck,

    Write them on the tablet of your heart.

4   So you will find favor and good repute
     In the sight of God and man.

5   Trust in the LORD with all your heart
     And do not lean on your own understanding.

6   In all your ways acknowledge Him,
     And He will make your paths straight.

7   Do not be wise in your own eyes;
     Fear the LORD and turn away from evil.

8   It will be healing to your body
     And refreshment to your bones.

9   Honor the LORD from your wealth
     And from the first of all your produce;

10   So your barns will be filled with plenty
     And your vats will overflow with new wine.

11   My son, do not reject the discipline of the LORD
     Or loathe His reproof,

12   For whom the LORD loves He reproves,
     Even as a father *corrects* the son in whom he delights.

21   My son, let them not vanish from your sight;
     Keep sound wisdom and discretion,

22   So they will be life to your soul
     And adornment to your neck.

Discuss with your GROUP or PONDER on your own . . .

What is the son to do with his father's commandments and what outcomes can he generally expect?

What causes you to forget? How can we keep kindness and truth from leaving?

Proverb ≠ Promise

My heart breaks when I hear people claim proverbs as promises which sets them up for profound disappointment. When God makes a covenant, a solemn binding agreement, He *always* keeps it! We see examples of God making covenants throughout His Word: He promises that Eve's seed will crush the head of the serpent; He promises never to destroy the earth again with a flood; He promises that a Son of David will sit on a forever throne; He promises to replace hearts of stone with hearts of flesh. These are covenants, promises that will never change.

Proverbs, though, are not promises. Proverbs are short sayings that generally prove true. "Train up a child in the way he should go, even when he is old he will not depart from it" (Proverbs 22:6) is a saying that generally proves true. The proverb encourages parents to fulfill their God-given responsibilities but doesn't guarantee specific results. We obey and trust God with the outcome. Our training can't save them; only God can do that!

Savvy
GOD'S TRUTH FOR A LIFE THAT WORKS

How is the son (and we readers) to respond to God and what will He do? (Look at where you marked LORD in verses 5-12; you'll see a pattern.)

ONE STEP FURTHER:

Discipline

If you have time this week, check out Hebrews 12:4-13 and see what it has to say about God's discipline. Record your findings below.

Then consider and reflect on a time when God disciplined you and recall what you learned.

How does your relationship to God and His Word compare with the Proverbs 3 instructions?

Now, take a look at the "do nots" in this section. List the common behaviors they warn against. Do you see any differences between the "do nots" of the first half of the chapter and those in verses 27-31? If so, explain what you noticed.

How does human wisdom/understanding fight with God's? Can you tell when it is happening in your life? If so, how?

According to Proverbs 3:11-12, what does God's discipline tell you about His disposition? How should this affect your response to reproof? How is that going?

According to Proverbs 3:13-26 in what ways is a wise person blessed?

How does the content shift beginning at verse 27?

How are the "devious" (Hebrew: *luz*) described in verse 32?

By contrast, what kind of relationship do the upright have with the LORD?

How does He relate to or deal with each?

Observe PROVERBS 4

READ Proverbs 4 and **MARK** the *wise* word group (*wisdom, understanding, discernment, knowledge,* etc.)

Proverbs 4

1 Hear, *O* sons, the instruction of a father,

And give attention that you may gain understanding,

2 For I give you sound teaching;

Do not abandon my instruction.

3 When I was a son to my father,

Tender and the only son in the sight of my mother,

4 Then he taught me and said to me,

"Let your heart hold fast my words;

Keep my commandments and live;

5 Acquire wisdom! Acquire understanding!

Do not forget nor turn away from the words of my mouth.

6 "Do not forsake her, and she will guard you;

Love her, and she will watch over you.

7 "The beginning of wisdom *is:* Acquire wisdom;

And with all your acquiring, get understanding.

8 "Prize her, and she will exalt you;

She will honor you if you embrace her.

9 "She will place on your head a garland of grace;

She will present you with a crown of beauty."

10 Hear, my son, and accept my sayings

And the years of your life will be many.

11 I have directed you in the way of wisdom;

I have led you in upright paths.

FYI:

Confidential Counsel

The word "intimate" in Proverbs 3:32 (NASB) translates the Hebrew *sod*, a word that suggests confidence and confidentiality between people. See also Jeremiah 23:18 and Amos 3:7.

Three times in Proverbs it's associated with keeping secrets. See Proverbs 11:13, 20:19, and 25:9.

INDUCTIVE PRINCIPLES:

Marking Time Phrases

If you're not in the habit of marking time phrases, now's a great time to start! I circle time phrases in green, but you can use any color or symbol you want; just try to maintain consistency.

Savvy

GOD'S TRUTH FOR A LIFE THAT WORKS

ONE STEP FURTHER:

Aquire Wisdom!

Take some time this week to identify the Hebrew word translated "acquire" in Proverbs 4:5 and 7. Then, check out how it is used in other places in Proverbs and elsewhere in the Old Testament. Record what you discover below.

12 When you walk, your steps will not be impeded;
And if you run, you will not stumble.

13 Take hold of instruction; do not let go.
Guard her, for she is your life.

14 Do not enter the path of the wicked
And do not proceed in the way of evil men.

15 Avoid it, do not pass by it;
Turn away from it and pass on.

16 For they cannot sleep unless they do evil;
And they are robbed of sleep unless they make *someone* stumble.

17 For they eat the bread of wickedness
And drink the wine of violence.

18 But the path of the righteous is like the light of dawn,
That shines brighter and brighter until the full day.

19 The way of the wicked is like darkness;
They do not know over what they stumble.

20 My son, give attention to my words;
Incline your ear to my sayings.

21 Do not let them depart from your sight;
Keep them in the midst of your heart.

22 For they are life to those who find them
And health to all their body.

23 Watch over your heart with all diligence,
For from it *flow* the springs of life.

24 Put away from you a deceitful mouth
And put devious speech far from you.

25 Let your eyes look directly ahead
And let your gaze be fixed straight in front of you.

26 Watch the path of your feet
And all your ways will be established.

27 Do not turn to the right nor to the left; Turn your foot from evil.

Discuss with your GROUP or PONDER on your own . . .

What did you learn by **marking** the *wisdom* word group? Look back at your markings and make a simple list. You can divide the list by the specific words or group them together. Be sure to include the verse references.

Summarize what Proverbs 4 teaches about wisdom and wise people.

a Closer Look

READ Proverbs 4:1-10 again and **MARK** the word *acquire*. The father and son in this section are significant. Watch for the change of speaker.

Proverbs 4:1-10

1 Hear, *O* sons, the instruction of a father,

   And give attention that you may gain understanding,

2 For I give you sound teaching;

   Do not abandon my instruction.

3 When I was a son to my father,

   Tender and the only son in the sight of my mother,

4 Then he taught me and said to me,

   "Let your heart hold fast my words;

   Keep my commandments and live;

5 Acquire wisdom! Acquire understanding!

   Do not forget nor turn away from the words of my mouth.

6 "Do not forsake her, and she will guard you;

   Love her, and she will watch over you.

7 "The beginning of wisdom *is:* Acquire wisdom;

   And with all your acquiring, get understanding.

8 "Prize her, and she will exalt you;

   She will honor you if you embrace her.

9 "She will place on your head a garland of grace;

   She will present you with a crown of beauty."

10 Hear, my son, and accept my sayings

   And the years of your life will be many.

Discuss with your GROUP or PONDER on your own . . .

Let's reason together. Who wrote these proverbs? (If you don't remember, refer back to Proverbs 1:1. Who is the author speaking to?)

A THOUGHT FROM: *Pam*

Overwhelmed?

There have been times in my life when I have felt entirely overwhelmed by the need for wisdom. Faced with a difficult question or situation, I would seek wisdom in God's Word and in the wise counsel of God's people.

I was always stunned by how simple so many of my seemingly complex questions were to those who had walked with God and in His ways for longer than I had. I often thought, "I'll never have *that* kind of wisdom."

A few years ago, the strangest thing started happening. I began receiving more and more phone calls and texts of the "I-have-something-I-need-to-talk-about" variety and instead of finding myself stumped by the complexity as I once had been, I realized that setting out to acquire wisdom was beginning to bear fruit, that in resolving to walk with the wise, some wisdom was finally growing in me.

If you pursue wisdom, if you seek God through His Word and ask for it, if you walk with the wise, my friend, be encouraged: one day you will be wise.

Savvy
GOD'S TRUTH FOR A LIFE THAT WORKS

What time in the past does he reference? (Marking time phrases helps us see this.)

A THOUGHT
FROM: *Pam*

Smart ≠ Wise

The older I get (and I'm not *that* old yet!), the more I realize that intellectual prowess does not always translate into practical results. The wisest people I know are not the smartest people I know—although they are plenty bright—and the smartest people I know don't always apply their knowledge well.

True wisdom doesn't come from books; wisdom comes from God through His Book and His Spirit.

Who taught him? What did he repeatedly say to acquire and why?

What does he assure his son of if he keeps wisdom and pays attention to his teaching? Why do you think this is important?

Do we run similar risks of abandoning truth today? If so, how and how can we guard against it?

What subject does the writer shift to in verse 10?

Savvy

What does Solomon command his son in verses 10-13? (Watch for imperative verbs.)

What does he warn against in verses 14-19?

How do these two ways of life contrast?

What does Solomon say about the ear, the heart, the eyes, the mouth, and the feet in verses 20-27?

Which of these need most attention in your life and why?

ONE STEP FURTHER:

History Books

If you have some extra time this week, read up on the circumstances surrounding Solomon's birth in 2 Samuel 11–12 and Psalm 51. Record your observations below as well as any questions that arise.

A THOUGHT FROM:

Processing Wisdom

The longer I live, the more I realize the influence of my parents. They made the most out of rugged circumstances and in the process they acquired wisdom. I can't remember them ever setting me down for "wisdom" lessons, but listening to them talk at the dinner table was my greatest place of learning.

I learned about relationships in the workplace as they spoke of their interaction with colleagues. I learned about work ethics and appropriate behavior as they spoke of their jobs. I also learned about interactions with extended family as they talked about "letters and long distance calls." Today, they might have referenced e-mails and texts, but the learning wasn't in the method, it was in the rich understanding I received as they talked.

Do you have a place where your children hear you "process wisdom"? Do you make regular times to be together with those you want to influence? Being intentional is one way to make provision to pass on the important things in life.

Digging Deeper

A Wise Father and Son

Take some time to examine the lives of David and Solomon. Use your concordance to find where each of them shows up in the Bible, and then begin some independent study. Just get a start today. There will be more time to add to this in weeks to come.

Significant Passages about David:

Key Points I Discovered:

Significant Passages about Solomon:

Key Points I Discovered:

@THE END OF THE DAY . . .

Take a few minutes to think and pray about what you've learned this week. Then summarize key truths you learned below. Before you finish, write one-sentence summaries describing Proverbs 2, 3, and 4. Then give each a simple hashtag.

Proverbs 2

One-Sentence Summary

Proverbs 3

One-Sentence Summary

Proverbs 4

One-Sentence Summary

Lesson Three
Around the Edges . . . A Father's Influence

. . . she gave birth to a son, and he named him Solomon. Now the LORD loved him and sent word through Nathan the prophet, and he named him Jedidiah for the LORD's sake.

−2 Samuel 12:24b-25

It's one thing to know what wisdom and foolishness do and don't do in theory. It's easy to say wise people listen and foolish people don't. Wise people listen to good counsel and foolish people don't. The facts are true but examples from lives help us to better understand the implications and nuances of lives lived wisely or foolishly.

This week we'll peek around the edges of Proverbs to see if we can discover why, when God said "Ask what *you wish* me to give you," Solomon chose wisdom. We'll also begin to see how Solomon and those close to him exhibit vibrant examples of both wise and foolish living.

ONE STEP FURTHER:

How Old Was Solomon?

If you're up for a challenge this week, see what you can find out about Solomon's age when he ascended the throne. Take into account how old David likely was when he was born, how old his brothers were, etc. There is no simple answer to this question, but see what you can put together from the facts God gives us in His Word.

From the Life of Solomon

In our study last week, we discovered that King David, the man after God's own heart, instructed his son Solomon to get wisdom. This week we'll look at other times when David told Solomon to act wisely and then see how Solomon chose wisdom for himself. Before we jump in, though, let's take a little time to review.

FYI:

The Brothers . . .
By the time King David appoints Solomon king, two of Solomon's older brothers have already failed in attempts to seize the throne.

LET'S REVIEW

What are the main points you recall from Proverbs 1–4?

What truths have you been applying so far?

What has been the easiest? What has been the hardest?

Have you noticed any changes in your life as you've been applying God's Word? Explain.

The Charge

Our first snapshot finds the kingdom of Israel in disarray. Solomon's older brother has just tried to seize the throne, but aging King David has been apprised of the situation and intervenes to establish Solomon as king in his place. Solomon has rivals, David has enemies, and keeping the peace will require a heavy dose of wisdom in the form of political savvy. Before David dies, he charges Solomon with the words below.

Observe the TEXT of SCRIPTURE

READ 1 Kings 2:1-10 and **MARK** *wisdom* and *wise*.

1 Kings 2:1-10

1 As David's time to die drew near, he charged Solomon his son, saying,

2 "I am going the way of all the earth. Be strong, therefore, and show yourself a man.

3 "Keep the charge of the LORD your God, to walk in His ways, to keep His statutes, His commandments, His ordinances, and His testimonies, according to what is written in the Law of Moses, that you may succeed in all that you do and wherever you turn,

4 so that the LORD may carry out His promise which He spoke concerning me, saying, 'If your sons are careful of their way, to walk before Me in truth with all their heart and with all their soul, you shall not lack a man on the throne of Israel.'

5 "Now you also know what Joab the son of Zeruiah did to me, what he did to the two commanders of the armies of Israel, to Abner the son of Ner, and to Amasa the son of Jether, whom he killed; he also shed the blood of war in peace. And he put the blood of war on his belt about his waist, and on his sandals on his feet.

6 "So act according to your wisdom, and do not let his gray hair go down to Sheol in peace.

7 "But show kindness to the sons of Barzillai the Gileadite, and let them be among those who eat at your table; for they assisted me when I fled from Absalom your brother.

8 "Behold, there is with you Shimei the son of Gera the Benjamite, of Bahurim; now it was he who cursed me with a violent curse on the day I went to Mahanaim. But when he came down to me at the Jordan, I swore to him by the LORD, saying, 'I will not put you to death with the sword.'

9 "Now therefore, do not let him go unpunished, for you are a wise man; and you will know what you ought to do to him, and you will bring his gray hair down to Sheol with blood."

10 Then David slept with his fathers and was buried in the city of David.

A THOUGHT FROM:

Brad, You're Going to Be a GREAT Driver

When my son was just a small boy, my mom would regularly say to him, "Brad, you're going to be a great driver!" I thought to myself, "Clearly my mom was never the mother of a son!"

Mostly I laughed under my breath when she said this, but because it happened so often, I finally had to remind her of how teenage boys actually drive. I also reminded her that her son-in-law had earned the name "Jehu" at least once during his teenage years!

Her response showed her wisdom as she told me that when Brad was old enough to drive, she wanted him always to remember his grandma telling him that she thought he would be a great driver so that if he felt inclined to do something not-so-wise, he'd think twice to not let Grandma down!

I wonder if David was doing the same thing with Solomon!

Savvy

GOD'S TRUTH FOR A LIFE THAT WORKS

FYI:

Dreams
The author of Hebrews tells us that God spoke "to the fathers in the prophets in many portions and in many ways." Dreams were one of those ways.

Discuss with your **GROUP** or **PONDER** on your own . . .

Describe the setting. Who is present and what is about to happen?

What does David tell Solomon to do and why?

What specifically is he to do with regard to the LORD His God? How will it benefit him?

How does David refer to Solomon in verse 9?

How will being wise benefit Solomon in difficult situations?

Are you facing any perplexing life situations? What questions are at the top of your mind with regard to your situation?

Savvy
GOD'S TRUTH FOR A LIFE THAT WORKS

How can wisdom benefit you?

How can you apply the wisdom that you are discovering from God's Word? Be as specific as possible.

The Offer and the Ask

God makes an amazing offer to Solomon in our next snapshot.

Observe the TEXT of SCRIPTURE

READ 1 Kings 3:3-9 and **MARK** *wisdom* and *wise*. Also **MARK** every occurrence of *Solomon*. As always, be sure to include pronouns.

1 Kings 3:3-9

3 Now Solomon loved the LORD, walking in the statutes of his father David, except he sacrificed and burned incense on the high places.

4 The king went to Gibeon to sacrifice there, for that was the great high place; Solomon offered a thousand burnt offerings on that altar.

5 In Gibeon the LORD appeared to Solomon in a dream at night; and God said, "Ask what *you wish* me to give you."

6 Then Solomon said, "You have shown great lovingkindness to Your servant David my father, according as he walked before You in truth and righteousness and uprightness of heart toward You; and You have reserved for him this great lovingkindness, that You have given him a son to sit on his throne, as *it is* this day.

7 "Now, O LORD my God, You have made Your servant king in place of my father David, yet I am but a little child; I do not know how to go out or come in.

8 "Your servant is in the midst of Your people which You have chosen, a great people who are too many to be numbered or counted.

9 "So give Your servant an understanding heart to judge Your people to discern between good and evil. For who is able to judge this great people of Yours?"

$\mathcal{D}$*iscuss* with your GROUP or PONDER on your own . . .

What is Solomon's disposition toward the LORD at this point in his life? Where do you see evidence of this?

How does his behavior compare with that of his father David?

Why is Solomon at Gibeon? What happens while he is there?

If God told you to ask Him for something, what would you ask for? Why?

What do you think most people would ask for? Again, why?

How does Solomon respond? How does he view himself? How does this compare with what David charged him in 1 Kings 2:2?

FYI:

Live Long and Prosper

Now this is the commandment, the statutes and the judgments which the LORD your God has commanded me to teach you, that you might do them in the land where you are going over to possess it, so that you and your son and your grandson might fear the LORD your God, to keep all His statutes and His commandments which I command you, all the days of your life, and that your days may be prolonged.

—Deuteronomy 6:1-2

GOD'S TRUTH FOR A LIFE THAT WORKS

What does he ask for? Be careful with this one; answer directly from the text.

The Answer

Solomon makes his request and God answers.

Observe the TEXT of SCRIPTURE

READ 1 Kings 3:10-15 and MARK *asked* and *wise*. Also MARK every reference to *God*, being sure to include synonyms and pronouns.

1 Kings 3:10-15

10 It was pleasing in the sight of the Lord that Solomon had asked this thing.

11 God said to him, "Because you have asked this thing and have not asked for yourself long life, nor have asked riches for yourself, nor have you asked for the life of your enemies, but have asked for yourself discernment to understand justice,

12 behold, I have done according to your words. Behold, I have given you a wise and discerning heart, so that there has been no one like you before you, nor shall one like you arise after you.

13 "I have also given you what you have not asked, both riches and honor, so that there will not be any among the kings like you all your days.

14 "If you walk in My ways, keeping My statutes and commandments, as your father David walked, then I will prolong your days."

15 Then Solomon awoke, and behold, it was a dream. And he came to Jerusalem and stood before the ark of the covenant of the Lord, and offered burnt offerings and made peace offerings, and made a feast for all his servants.

Discuss with your GROUP or PONDER on your own . . .

How does God respond to Solomon's request?

A THOUGHT FROM: JAN

Everything Except...
Did you ever have a child say to you, "I did everything you told me, except..."? Usually the "except" was bigger than he described, but for him the "except" was just a small thing that really didn't matter. "I know you told me to clean my room and I did, except I didn't make up my bed."

The "excepts" in life always dangle about as excuses for the things we've either done "in exception" or not done "in exception" to instruction. Either way, the exceptions we make for ourselves can be mighty.

A wise person knows how easy it is to "except" himself from God's ways. Just as Solomon walked in the ways of the Lord "except," we've all seen what those exceptions can do in our own lives.

Savvy
GOD'S TRUTH FOR A LIFE THAT WORKS

How does He describe what Solomon asked for? Is this more narrow than what is typically attributed to him?

FYI:

Asking according to God's will

This is the confidence which we have before Him, that, if we ask anything according to His will, He hears us. And if we know that He hears us in whatever we ask, we know that we have the requests which we have asked from Him.

—1 John 5:14-15

What else does God give Solomon? Why?

What does God tell Solomon to do to prolong his days? Do you think this fits in with his having a wise and discerning heart? As always, answer from the text.

Do you think wisdom and disobedience coexisted in Solomon? Why/why not?

How does Solomon respond in the moment?

If God was so pleased to give wisdom to Solomon, do you think He would be pleased to give it to you? Explain your answer.

If you've never asked God for wisdom, what is holding you back?

Savvy
GOD'S TRUTH FOR A LIFE THAT WORKS

Digging Deeper

David Asked for One Thing, Too

Take some extra time this week to check out Psalm 27. You'll discover there the one thing David asked God for.

Briefly summarize Psalm 27.

What is the "one thing" David asked for?

How does David's "one thing" compare with Solomon's request? Use Scripture to back up your view.

The Evidence

Everybody sees and acknowledges Solomon's wisdom to rule!

Observe the TEXT of SCRIPTURE

READ 1 Kings 3:16-28 and **MARK** *king*. As always, include synonyms and pronouns.

1 Kings 3:16-28

16 Then two women who were harlots came to the king and stood before him.

17 The one woman said, "Oh, my lord, this woman and I live in the same house; and I gave birth to a child while she *was* in the house.

18 "It happened on the third day after I gave birth, that this woman also gave birth to a child, and we were together. There was no stranger with us in the house, only the two of us in the house.

19 "This woman's son died in the night, because she lay on it.

20 "So she arose in the middle of the night and took my son from beside me while your maidservant slept, and laid him in her bosom, and laid her dead son in my bosom.

21 "When I rose in the morning to nurse my son, behold, he was dead; but when I looked at him carefully in the morning, behold, he was not my son, whom I had borne."

22 Then the other woman said, "No! For the living one is my son, and the dead one is your son." But the first woman said, "No! For the dead one is your son, and the living one is my son." Thus they spoke before the king.

23 Then the king said, "The one says, 'This is my son who is living, and your son is the dead one'; and the other says, 'No! For your son is the dead one, and my son is the living one.' "

24 The king said, "Get me a sword." So they brought a sword before the king.

25 The king said, "Divide the living child in two, and give half to the one and half to the other."

26 Then the woman whose child *was* the living one spoke to the king, for she was deeply stirred over her son and said, "Oh, my lord, give her the living child, and by no means kill him." But the other said, "He shall be neither mine nor yours; divide *him!*"

27 Then the king said, "Give the first woman the living child, and by no means kill him. She is his mother."

28 When all Israel heard of the judgment which the king had handed down, they feared the king, for they saw that the wisdom of God was in him to administer justice.

Discuss with your GROUP or PONDER on your own . . .

Describe the situation Solomon faces with the two harlots.

What is the claim of Harlot #1?

How does Harlot #2's claim compare?

Have you ever been in a similar situation where you know someone is lying? If so, describe it. Were you able to get to the truth? If so, how did you do it?

How does Solomon resolve the conflict? How does he cause the truth to surface when he *knows* someone is lying?

How do the women respond?

What effect does this have on the nation? What do they recognize in him?

What effect do you think a ruler with "the wisdom of God . . . to administer justice" would have on the nation you live in?

Given all the benefits Solomon had, what trajectory would you expect his life to take? Would you expect him to finish well or poorly? Why?

@THE END OF THE DAY . . .

Take some time to reflect on what you've learned this week about Solomon and the wisdom that God gave him. If you haven't asked God for wisdom before now, today is a good day to do it!

Lesson Four
The Wicked Dies For Lack of Instruction

His own iniquities will capture the wicked,
And he will be held with the cords of his sin.
He will die for lack of instruction,
And in the greatness of his folly he will go astray.
—Proverbs 5:22-23

There are times when it seems that the guilty will walk free forever—days when the arrogant stare down from the towers they've built on the backs of innocents by way of their wicked plans, lying tongues, and blood-stained hands. Their lives seem sweet and smooth . . . exhilarating even, as they chart their own courses and please themselves, flouting every voice that warns. Does it gnaw at you when life seems to smile on the wicked as they skip along in rebellion? God give us compassion for these as they blindly career toward destruction.

 PROVERBS 1–4

Take a few minutes to think back over what we've studied so far. Be sure to include both *what you've been learning* and *how you've been applying* what you've learned.

Proverbs 1

Proverbs 2

Proverbs 3

Proverbs 4

 SOLOMON'S LIFE

Record your biggest application point from studying Solomon's life so far. What benefits did he have? Let's keep these in mind as we continue to study.

Observe Proverbs 5

READ Proverbs 5 and **UNDERLINE** every direct command. Then **MARK** every word that refers to the *adulteress woman*. Be sure to include other synonyms and pronouns as appropriate.

Proverbs 5

1 My son, give attention to my wisdom,

Incline your ear to my understanding;

2 That you may observe discretion

And your lips may reserve knowledge.

3 For the lips of an adulteress drip honey

And smoother than oil is her speech;

4 But in the end she is bitter as wormwood,

Sharp as a two-edged sword.

5 Her feet go down to death,

Her steps take hold of Sheol.

6 She does not ponder the path of life;

Her ways are unstable, she does not know *it*.

7 Now then, *my* sons, listen to me

And do not depart from the words of my mouth.

8 Keep your way far from her

And do not go near the door of her house,

9 Or you will give your vigor to others

And your years to the cruel one;

10 And strangers will be filled with your strength

And your hard-earned goods *will go* to the house of an alien;

11 And you groan at your final end,

When your flesh and your body are consumed;

12 And you say, "How I have hated instruction!

And my heart spurned reproof!

13 "I have not listened to the voice of my teachers,

Nor inclined my ear to my instructors!

14 "I was almost in utter ruin

In the midst of the assembly and congregation."

15 Drink water from your own cistern

And fresh water from your own well.

16 Should your springs be dispersed abroad,

Streams of water in the streets?

17 Let them be yours alone

And not for strangers with you.

18 Let your fountain be blessed,

And rejoice in the wife of your youth.

19 *As* a loving hind and a graceful doe,

Let her breasts satisfy you at all times;

Be exhilarated always with her love.

20 For why should you, my son, be exhilarated with an adulteress

And embrace the bosom of a foreigner?

21 For the ways of a man are before the eyes of the LORD,

And He watches all his paths.

22 His own iniquities will capture the wicked,

And he will be held with the cords of his sin.

23 He will die for lack of instruction,

And in the greatness of his folly he will go astray.

A THOUGHT FROM:

Tried it yet?

Have you tried marking in your Bible yet? If you're hesitant, get yourself some erasable pens. The ability to erase takes the pressure off! So go ahead and give it a try unless marking gives you hives. Remember, if it gives you hives, just mark in the workbook.

FYI:

Psalm 119:103-104

While Proverbs 5:3 says that the lips of an adulteress drip honey, the psalmist assures us that God's Word is sweeter than honey and that it *keeps* him from false ways . . . like that of the adulteress! Check it out:

How sweet are Your words to my taste!
Yes, sweeter than honey to my mouth!
From Your precepts I get understanding;
Therefore I hate every false way.

—Psalm 119:103-104

Savvy

GOD'S TRUTH FOR A LIFE THAT WORKS

FYI:

The Double-Edged Sword

The lips of the adulteress, according to Proverbs 5:4 are sharp as a two-edged sword in a negative sense . . . she leads people to death. Contrast this with the words of Hebrews where we are told about the piercing Word of God that works for good in our lives. Check it out:

12 For the word of God is living and active and sharper than any two-edged sword, and piercing as far as the division of soul and spirit, of both joints and marrow, and able to judge the thoughts and intentions of the heart.

13 And there is no creature hidden from His sight, but all things are open and laid bare to the eyes of Him with whom we have to do.

14 Therefore, since we have a great high priest who has passed through the heavens, Jesus the Son of God, let us hold fast our confession.

15 For we do not have a high priest who cannot sympathize with our weaknesses, but One who has been tempted in all things as we are, yet without sin.

16 Therefore let us draw near with confidence to the throne of grace, so that we may receive mercy and find grace to help in time of need.

—Hebrews 4:12-16

Discuss with your GROUP or PONDER on your own . . .

How will paying attention to his father's wisdom benefit the son?

Look back at every command word or phrase you underlined, then list:

The positive commands   **The negative commands**

What main wisdom categories does Proverbs 5 address? What specific topics?

Describe the adulteress. Why is she desirable? What is she like?

What happens to those involved with her?

Do you think this is a metaphor or is Solomon speaking specifically of sexual fidelity in marriage? Explain your answer.

How do you think Solomon's life would have differed had he heeded his own counsel in Proverbs 5:18?

What is the condition of the person who doesn't listen to instruction? (See vv. 11-14, 22-23.)

a Closer Look

READ Proverbs 5:21-23 and **MARK** the references to being *captured* or *held*.

Proverbs 5:21-23

21 For the ways of a man are before the eyes of the LORD,
   And He watches all his paths.

22 His own iniquities will capture the wicked,
   And he will be held with the cords of his sin.

23 He will die for lack of instruction,
   And in the greatness of his folly he will go astray.

Discuss with your GROUP or PONDER on your own . . .

What does Solomon say will capture and hold the wicked?

What will eventually happen to him? What "lack" will cause it?

ONE STEP FURTHER:

Word Study: Adulteress
Take some time this week to examine the words translated "adulteress" in Proverbs 5:20. Use blueletterbible.com or another concordance tool to uncover the original Hebrew word. Then use the concordance to see how the Hebrew word is typically translated. Record your observations below.

Savvy
GOD'S TRUTH FOR A LIFE THAT WORKS

ONE STEP FURTHER:

Foreign Wives

Take some time this week to compare Solomon's personal life to his instructions. Use your concordance and some elbow grease to find the answers to the questions that follow. As you study, consider the implications for Solomon and for those who follow his ways instead of his words.

- *How many wives did Solomon have?*

- *How many other women?*

- *Where did these women come from?*

- *Who did these women worship?*

- *What effect did these relationships have on Solomon?*

A THOUGHT FROM: *Pam*

Sobered

I'm sobered when I consider Solomon's life. Clearly, he knew God's Word. Clearly, that Word was delivered to him with care. Still, though he possessed every opportunity and knew the path to walk, he often chose to walk his own way in his own considerable power. The queen of Sheba and the rest of the world thought he was on top of the world, but God who judges the thoughts and intents of the heart knew differently. Anyone paying attention to the revealed Word of God would have known that Solomon's rejection of God's commands in Deuteronomy 17:14-20 would be his ultimate undoing.

Solomon may have ruled the people well, but he ruled his own life dismally.

Digging Deeper

Song of Solomon

Scholars disagree over the interpretation of Song of Solomon. If you have some extra time this week, read the book (only eight chapters) and then research the varying interpretations of this wisdom literature attributed to Solomon. To do this, you'll want a commentary that explains various viewpoints. One such commentary is *The New American Commentary: Proverbs, Ecclesiastes, Song of Songs.*

Observations from Song of Solomon:

Scholarly views that I discovered:

My takeaways after reading Song of Solomon and interacting with the scholarly views:

Observe Proverbs 6

READ Proverbs 6 and **MARK** references to negative behaviors or traits (*sluggard, wicked, adulteress*, etc.). Be sure to include other synonyms and pronouns as appropriate.

Proverbs 6

1 My son, if you have become surety for your neighbor,

Have given a pledge for a stranger,

2 *If* you have been snared with the words of your mouth,

Have been caught with the words of your mouth,

3 Do this then, my son, and deliver yourself;

Since you have come into the hand of your neighbor,

Go, humble yourself, and importune your neighbor.

4 Give no sleep to your eyes,

Nor slumber to your eyelids;

5 Deliver yourself like a gazelle from *the hunter's* hand

And like a bird from the hand of the fowler.

6 Go to the ant, O sluggard,

Observe her ways and be wise,

7 Which, having no chief,

Officer or ruler,

8 Prepares her food in the summer

And gathers her provision in the harvest.

9 How long will you lie down, O sluggard?

When will you arise from your sleep?

10 "A little sleep, a little slumber, A little folding of the hands to rest"—

11 Your poverty will come in like a vagabond

And your need like an armed man.

12 A worthless person, a wicked man,

Is the one who walks with a perverse mouth,

13 Who winks with his eyes, who signals with his feet,

Who points with his fingers;

14 Who *with* perversity in his heart continually devises evil,

Who spreads strife.

15 Therefore his calamity will come suddenly;

Instantly he will be broken and there will be no healing.

16 There are six things which the LORD hates,

Yes, seven which are an abomination to Him:

17 Haughty eyes, a lying tongue,

And hands that shed innocent blood,

18 A heart that devises wicked plans,

Feet that run rapidly to evil,

19 A false witness *who* utters lies,

And one who spreads strife among brothers.

20 My son, observe the commandment of your father

And do not forsake the teaching of your mother;

21 Bind them continually on your heart;

Tie them around your neck.

22 When you walk about, they will guide you;

When you sleep, they will watch over you;

And when you awake, they will talk to you.

ONE STEP FURTHER:

Word Study: Perverse
Take some time this week to explore the words "perverse" (6:12) and "perversity" (6:14). Identify the Hebrew roots and compare them with one another. Also see how else they are used throughout the Word of God. Record your findings below.

Savvy

GOD'S TRUTH FOR A LIFE THAT WORKS

FYI:

The Engine

If we look at the proverbs as grit-yer-teeth-and-get-'em-done imperatives to carry out by the strength of our backs and the sweat of our brows, we will live in eventual discouragement and failure.

If we realize, though, that the wisdom-filled life is possible not by our own efforts, but by the Holy Spirit who dwells within, we can learn some specifics, some tactics if you will, to help us live well.

The Holy Spirit is the engine that powers the wise life described in the proverbs.

FYI:

Covenants

Covenants are solemn, binding agreements between two parties. If you and I make a covenant together, your enemies become my enemies and my enemies become yours. Think about how many marriage covenants Solomon entered. Although he had plenty of power and money, he was a man bound to many covenant partners.

23 For the commandment is a lamp and the teaching is light;
And reproofs for discipline are the way of life

24 To keep you from the evil woman,
From the smooth tongue of the adulteress.

25 Do not desire her beauty in your heart,
Nor let her capture you with her eyelids.

26 For on account of a harlot *one is reduced* to a loaf of bread,
And an adulteress hunts for the precious life.

27 Can a man take fire in his bosom
And his clothes not be burned?

28 Or can a man walk on hot coals
And his feet not be scorched?

29 So is the one who goes in to his neighbor's wife;
Whoever touches her will not go unpunished.

30 Men do not despise a thief if he steals
To satisfy himself when he is hungry;

31 But when he is found, he must repay sevenfold;
He must give all the substance of his house.

32 The one who commits adultery with a woman is lacking sense;
He who would destroy himself does it.

33 Wounds and disgrace he will find,
And his reproach will not be blotted out.

34 For jealousy enrages a man,
And he will not spare in the day of vengeance.

35 He will not accept any ransom,
Nor will he be satisfied though you give many gifts.

a Closer Look

READ Proverbs 6:1-5 again and **MARK** every the reference to being *captured* or *held*.

Proverbs 6:1-5

1 My son, if you have become surety for your neighbor,
Have given a pledge for a stranger,

2 *If* you have been snared with the words of your mouth,
Have been caught with the words of your mouth,

3 Do this then, my son, and deliver yourself;
Since you have come into the hand of your neighbor,
Go, humble yourself, and importune your neighbor.

4 Give no sleep to your eyes,
Nor slumber to your eyelids;

5 Deliver yourself like a gazelle from *the hunter's* hand
And like a bird from the hand of the fowler.

Savvy
GOD'S TRUTH FOR A LIFE THAT WORKS

Discuss with your GROUP or PONDER on your own . . .

At the end of Proverbs 5 we saw that a wicked man's own iniquities and sins will capture and hold him. According to Proverbs 6:1-5, what else can snare a person?

Can you think of any examples where Solomon might have been on the wrong end of surety?

What is an example of a "surety" situation today? Have you ever had a loan or guaranteed someone else's? Explain.

What does Solomon counsel? What actions does this involve?

If you are in this situation, what actions will you need to take to remove yourself?

A THOUGHT FROM:

Bailing People Out

Friends, I've come a long way over the past 25 years. There was a time I would give you the credit card off my back! In trouble? Let me help, I've got a credit line.

I know, some of you are shaking your heads with me because you've done the same thing. Others are swinging your heads back and forth because you've never been this foolish!

It's one thing to bail someone out when you have the means and you are ready to simply pay the bill. It is another thing to guarantee a payment or assume payment when you do not have the means. Today, because of our credit mentality, it's easy to think we have the money when we don't.

Generosity is close to the heart of God, but risky debt assumption is dangerous and usually downright stupid. I'm calling it what it is because I'm calling myself out for having done it. As my friend Jan Silvious often says, "An education is expensive and you get it in many ways." My education on this one cost me about $1,500 plus interest. Too bad I didn't pay attention to this proverb back then . . . who knows how much that could have turned into by today! Oh well, at least I've learned!

Savvy

GOD'S TRUTH FOR A LIFE THAT WORKS

According to Proverbs 6:6-8 what creature lives wisely? What does it do? What *doesn't* it need and why? What lesson can we learn from it?

By contrast, what does the sluggard do? What can the sluggard expect?

Are you more encouraged or goaded by this? Explain.

How well do you receive instruction? What have you learned over the years that has made listening easier for you?

Describe the wicked man in verses 12-14. What is he like and what does he do?

What can the wicked expect?

Let's look more at some sins God actually hates.

Read Proverbs 6:16-19 and **MARK** the seven abominations to God.

Proverbs 6:16-19

16 There are six things which the LORD hates,

Yes, seven which are an abomination to Him:

17 Haughty eyes, a lying tongue,

And hands that shed innocent blood,

18 A heart that devises wicked plans,

Feet that run rapidly to evil,

19 A false witness *who* utters lies,

And one who spreads strife among brothers.

Discuss with your **GROUP** or **PONDER** on your own . . .

What parts of the body are associated with things God hates?

Which ones have to do primarily with speaking?

Which have to do primarily with attitudes?

Which have to do primarily with actions?

A THOUGHT FROM:

Don't Go There!

"Keep it to yourself" is a worthy motto for the wise. It is so easy to stir up strife by telling a friend what another friend has said about her! It is easy to be a "stir stick" when you believe you have to say something if you know something. There are things that, if you're wise, you'll take to your grave. Some things just don't need to be shared! It takes maturity and a lot of wisdom "to know when to hold 'em and to know when to fold 'em." You can always say something later if really necessary, but you can't take your information back once you realize you have caused a problem!

There are topics and platforms that wise people avoid! Strife comes when people disagree. In our world, there are a lot of things about which to disagree but wisdom says "Don't go there!" Your opinion is not going to change anyone's mind. Social media is a hotbed for strife, and nothing is worse than seeing believers wrangling over politics. The anonymity of the Internet makes injecting opinions easy but the strife it can cause can divide friends and even make enemies of people you'll never know. "Keep it to yourself" is some of the best advice any of us can embrace! Whether in person or on social media, "keep it to yourself!" You won't regret it!

Savvy

GOD'S TRUTH FOR A LIFE THAT WORKS

ONE STEP FURTHER:

David/Bathsheba

As Solomon warns against adultery, remember that he was born in the shadow of his parents' adultery. His older brother, the product of David and Bathsheba's adultery, died as judgment on David's sin. Solomon saw firsthand the wounds that adultery brings. Check out the account for yourself in 2 Samuel 11-12. Record your observations below.

Do you recognize any of these in your life? Just asking . . .

What instructions does Solomon give starting in verse 20? (Watch the verbs.)

What specifics does he warn against? What potential consequences does he highlight?

How will these teachings and commandments benefit the son? How can they benefit *you* this week?

@THE END OF THE DAY . . .

Think back through what you've studied this week. Briefly summarize what you've learned so you can share it with someone.

Then, write one-sentence summaries describing Proverbs 5 and 6 so you can easily recall them. Finish by giving each chapter a hashtag "name."

Proverbs 5

One-Sentence Summary

Proverbs 6

One-Sentence Summary

This is the specific truth I'm going to focus on this week:

Women . . .

At the entrance of the doors, she cries out . . .
–Proverbs 8:3b

Lady wisdom calls, but she is not alone . . . another comes calling, too! In Proverbs 7 through 9, both wisdom and folly stand center stage personified as women who call out distinct messages to the naive and to those who lack understanding. Choosing which call to answer means the difference between life and death.

FYI:

Remember Genre?
Metaphors, personification, similes . . . are you flashing back to fifth grade language arts class?! Remember as we work through Proverbs, interpretation will require understanding these style genres that will appear from time to time.

Savvy
GOD'S TRUTH FOR A LIFE THAT WORKS

Review PROVERBS 1–6

Take a few minutes to think back over what we've studied so far. Be sure to include both *what you've been learning* and *how you've been applying* what you've learned.

Proverbs 1

Proverbs 2

Proverbs 3

Proverbs 4

Proverbs 5

Proverbs 6

Biggest overall takeaway so far:

Observe Proverbs 7

READ Proverbs 7 and **MARK** references to the *young man* and to the *woman* who comes out to meet him. Be sure to include synonyms and pronouns.

Proverbs 7

1 My son, keep my words
And treasure my commandments within you.

2 Keep my commandments and live,
And my teaching as the apple of your eye.

3 Bind them on your fingers;
Write them on the tablet of your heart.

4 Say to wisdom, "You are my sister,"
And call understanding *your* intimate friend;

5 That they may keep you from an adulteress,
From the foreigner who flatters with her words.

6 For at the window of my house
I looked out through my lattice,

7 And I saw among the naive,
And discerned among the youths
A young man lacking sense,

8 Passing through the street near her corner;
And he takes the way to her house,

9 In the twilight, in the evening,
In the middle of the night and *in* the darkness.

10 And behold, a woman *comes* to meet him,
Dressed as a harlot and cunning of heart.

11 She is boisterous and rebellious,
Her feet do not remain at home;

12 *She is* now in the streets, now in the squares,
And lurks by every corner.

13 So she seizes him and kisses him
And with a brazen face she says to him:

14 "I was due to offer peace offerings;
Today I have paid my vows.

15 "Therefore I have come out to meet you,
To seek your presence earnestly, and I have found you.

16 "I have spread my couch with coverings,
With colored linens of Egypt.

17 "I have sprinkled my bed
With myrrh, aloes and cinnamon.

18 "Come, let us drink our fill of love until morning;
Let us delight ourselves with caresses.

19 "For my husband is not at home,
He has gone on a long journey;

20 He has taken a bag of money with him,
At the full moon he will come home."

21 With her many persuasions she entices him;
With her flattering lips she seduces him.

22 Suddenly he follows her
As an ox goes to the slaughter,
Or as *one in* fetters to the discipline of a fool,

23 Until an arrow pierces through his liver;
As a bird hastens to the snare,
So he does not know that it *will cost him* his life.

Savvy
GOD'S TRUTH FOR A LIFE THAT WORKS

> 24 Now therefore, *my* sons, listen to me,
>   And pay attention to the words of my mouth.
> 25 Do not let your heart turn aside to her ways,
>   Do not stray into her paths.
>
> 26 For many are the victims she has cast down,
>   And numerous are all her slain.
> 27 Her house is the way to Sheol,
>   Descending to the chambers of death.

a Closer Look

READ Proverbs 7:1-5 again and **UNDERLINE** every instruction to the son.

Proverbs 7:1-5

1   My son, keep my words
     And treasure my commandments within you.

2   Keep my commandments and live,
     And my teaching as the apple of your eye.

3   Bind them on your fingers;
     Write them on the tablet of your heart.

4   Say to wisdom, "You are my sister,"
     And call understanding *your* intimate friend;

5   That they may keep you from an adulteress,
     From the foreigner who flatters with her words.

Discuss with your GROUP or PONDER on your own . . .

List the instructions you underlined in Proverbs 7:1-5.

What teachings is the son to treasure? How will he do this?

These Words . . .

4 "Hear, O Israel! The LORD is our God, the LORD is one!

5 "You shall love the LORD your God with all your heart and with all your soul and with all your might.

6 "These words, which I am commanding you today, shall be on your heart.

7 "You shall teach them diligently to your sons and shall talk of them when you sit in your house and when you walk by the way and when you lie down and when you rise up.

8 "You shall bind them as a sign on your hand and they shall be as frontals on your forehead.

9 "You shall write them on the doorposts of your house and on your gates."

—Deuteronomy 6:4-9

What specific ways can you do this?

How can you help your children/grandchildren/others treasure God's commands?

What do you treasure as "the apple of your eye" or call "intimate friend"? What is closest to your heart? What do you guard most fiercely?

What risks do we face when something other than truth reigns in our hearts? Explain.

According to Proverbs 7:5 what will the word/commandment/teaching protect against?

Describe wisdom and understanding from verse 4. How should this impact a person's actions in the face of a flattering tempter or temptress?

ONE STEP FURTHER:

Word Studies

If you have time this week, examine the words used to describe the young man in Proverbs 7:6-9. See if you can find the Hebrew word each translates and then examine how each is used throughout Proverbs and the rest of the Old Testament.

Youth

Young Man

Naive

Lacking Sense

Savvy
GOD'S TRUTH FOR A LIFE THAT WORKS

A THOUGHT FROM:

Set up for Trouble

Proverbs 7 warns about sexual sin, specifically the allure of the adulteress, which is one snare in the greater anti-wisdom world. That said, I believe we miss out if we fail to connect the behavior of this particular antagonist to the fundamental way sin attacks.

As a middle-aged woman, I have to remind myself not to gloss over Proverbs 7. There is so much to learn about keeping ourselves from being "an accident waiting to happen" in every realm of life. Wisdom listens to the voice of instruction, not the smooth words of flatterers.

ONE STEP FURTHER:

Peace Offerings

Take some time to explore the peace offerings that the woman talks about. What were they? How often were they paid? How does this detail fit into the story? Record your finds below.

Questions on verses 6–9

Describe the young man. Where is he seen? When is he there? What is he doing?

Do you think he is an easy target for trouble? Why/why not?

Are there ways you "set *yourself* up" for trouble? If so, how? What corrective measures can you take?

Questions on verses 10-23

Describe the woman. Where is she?

What does she do? Watch the verbs in verses 12-13. (As you answer, remember Proverbs 7:5.)

How does the woman bait her trap?

What ultimately seduces the young man (v. 21)?

What metaphors describe his fate? What does his sin cost him?

Does this young man go knowingly? Why does he succumb?

 Read Proverbs 7:24-27 and, again, **UNDERLINE** every instruction to the son.

Proverbs 7:24-27

24   Now therefore, *my* sons, listen to me,

     And pay attention to the words of my mouth.

25   Do not let your heart turn aside to her ways,

     Do not stray into her paths.

26   For many are the victims she has cast down,

     And numerous are all her slain.

27   Her house is the way to Sheol,

     Descending to the chambers of death.

Discuss with your **GROUP** or **PONDER** on your own . . .

Where does the adulteress's path lead? Given this, how dangerous is the road?

What does the father tell his sons to do? How can we apply these today?

Digging Deeper

Treasure, Keep, Bind, Write

Take some time to investigate Psalm 119:9-16 (the Beth stanza) on your own to discover what the Psalmist says about keeping his way pure and what the Word of God has to do with it.

What does the stanza teach about God's Word (precepts, statutes, laws, testimonies, commandments, ordinances)?

What is the psalmist concerned to avoid?

What does the psalmist desire?

What does the psalmist ask God for? What does he resolve to do?

Summarize your main takeaways from Psalm 119:9-16.

ONE STEP FURTHER:

A Call to All

While the adulteress hunts one by one, wisdom originally calls to all! She stands by the gates and calls to anyone who will listen! James repeats this truth and encourages believers who lack wisdom to ask God for it, because He "gives to all generously." Take some time to read and reflect on James 1:5-8, then record below what you learned.

GOD'S TRUTH FOR A LIFE THAT WORKS

Observe Proverbs 8

READ and **MARK** *wisdom, God,* and any time phrases you notice in Proverbs 8. If you haven't tried marking your Bible yet, this is an easy chapter to start with. Don't go crazy; start by simply **MARKING** *wisdom* and all the associated pronouns. It's a good way to dip your toe in the water.

Proverbs 8

1 Does not wisdom call,

And understanding lift up her voice?

2 On top of the heights beside the way,

Where the paths meet, she takes her stand;

3 Beside the gates, at the opening to the city,

At the entrance of the doors, she cries out:

4 "To you, O men, I call,

And my voice is to the sons of men.

5 "O naive ones, understand prudence;

And, O fools, understand wisdom.

6 "Listen, for I will speak noble things;

And the opening of my lips *will reveal* right things.

7 "For my mouth will utter truth;

And wickedness is an abomination to my lips.

8 "All the utterances of my mouth are in righteousness;

There is nothing crooked or perverted in them.

9 "They are all straightforward to him who understands,

And right to those who find knowledge.

10 "Take my instruction and not silver,

And knowledge rather than choicest gold.

11 "For wisdom is better than jewels;

And all desirable things cannot compare with her.

12 "I, wisdom, dwell with prudence,

And I find knowledge *and* discretion.

13 "The fear of the LORD is to hate evil;

Pride and arrogance and the evil way

And the perverted mouth, I hate.

14 "Counsel is mine and sound wisdom;

I am understanding, power is mine.

15 "By me kings reign,

And rulers decree justice.

16 "By me princes rule, and nobles,

All who judge rightly.

17 "I love those who love me;

And those who diligently seek me will find me.

18 "Riches and honor are with me,

Enduring wealth and righteousness.

19 "My fruit is better than gold, even pure gold,

And my yield *better* than choicest silver.

20 "I walk in the way of righteousness,

In the midst of the paths of justice,

21 To endow those who love me with wealth,

That I may fill their treasuries.

22 "The LORD possessed me at the beginning of His way,

Before His works of old.

FYI:

The Very Great Reward

After these things the word of the LORD came to Abram in a vision, saying,

"Do not be afraid, Abram. I am your shield, your exceedingly great reward."

—Genesis 15:1, NKJV

Savvy

GOD'S TRUTH FOR A LIFE THAT WORKS

23 "From everlasting I was established,

From the beginning, from the earliest times of the earth.

24 "When there were no depths I was brought forth,

When there were no springs abounding with water.

25 "Before the mountains were settled,

Before the hills I was brought forth;

26 While He had not yet made the earth and the fields,

Nor the first dust of the world.

27 "When He established the heavens, I was there,

When He inscribed a circle on the face of the deep,

28 When He made firm the skies above,

When the springs of the deep became fixed,

29 When He set for the sea its boundary

So that the water would not transgress His command,

When He marked out the foundations of the earth;

30 Then I was beside Him, as a master workman;

And I was daily *His* delight,

Rejoicing always before Him,

31 Rejoicing in the world, His earth,

And *having* my delight in the sons of men.

32 "Now therefore, *O* sons, listen to me,

For blessed are they who keep my ways.

33 "Heed instruction and be wise,

And do not neglect *it*.

34 "Blessed is the man who listens to me,

Watching daily at my gates,

Waiting at my doorposts.

35 "For he who finds me finds life

And obtains favor from the LORD.

36 "But he who sins against me injures himself;

All those who hate me love death."

Discuss with your GROUP or PONDER on your own . . .

Look back at your markings and list everything you noted that wisdom does.

Where does she call from? What is the significance of the locations? How does this differ from the adulteress woman's call in Proverbs 7?

FYI:

Pure Words

*The words of the LORD are pure words;
as silver tried in a furnace on the earth,
refined seven times.*

—Psalm 12:6

Savvy

GOD'S TRUTH FOR A LIFE THAT WORKS

Who does she address? Is there hope for everyone? Why/why not?

What is needed to benefit from her?

What difference does truth make?

Can anything compare with wisdom? What comes with it according to the text? Does this give you pause? Why/why not? How does this integrate with New Testament teaching?

How is "the fear of the LORD" defined in verse 13? How does this compare with other uses of the phrase in Proverbs?

What else is associated with wisdom according to verse 14?

How is wisdom related to just rule of law?

God's Question to Job

There's biblical credibility attached to being present at creation. Wisdom was there but Job wasn't . . .

1   Then the LORD answered Job out of the whirlwind and said,

2   "Who is this that darkens counsel
    By words without knowledge?

3   "Now gird up your loins like a man,
    And I will ask you, and you instruct Me!

4   "Where were you when I laid the foundation of the earth?
    Tell Me, if you have understanding . . ."
                                —Job 38:1-4

How do people find wisdom? What else is typically with her?

Questions on verses 22-31

How long has wisdom existed? What did she witness?

What does this say about her importance and authority?

If God acted with wisdom (as the text says He did), what does this say about how much we should value her?

Questions on verses 32-36

How does the "therefore" in verse 32 relate to the content in verses 22-31?

Why should the father's sons listen to wisdom?

What practical choices do we have in the face of wisdom? Which do you typically choose? Why? What outcomes have you experienced?

What else comes with wisdom according to verse 35?

What can you expect if you sin against wisdom?

A THOUGHT FROM:  *Pam*

Invested

As far back as I can remember, I have sought out teachers and coaches to help me improve at whatever endeavor I was undertaking.

I'd like to say it was humble wisdom that prompted me, but more likely it was youthful pragmatism and a downright competitive edge. Why expend energy and effort on fruitless paths when others know the way and can help propel you along the path?

Some of those people have been paid—high school teachers and college professors who poured into me and yet drew a salary. Others, though, have truly *invested* in me—people wiser than I who have poured years of time and energy into helping me learn and increase in wisdom . . . and I *love* them. I wouldn't be who I am without their investment. Because I have been so heavily invested in, I've learned to likewise invest in others . . . and it is one of the great joys of my life!

How are you investing your life in others' lives?

Savvy
GOD'S TRUTH FOR A LIFE THAT WORKS

Observe Proverbs 9

READ Proverbs 9 and **MARK** in a distinctive way the references to *wisdom* and *folly*.

Proverbs 9

1 Wisdom has built her house,
   She has hewn out her seven pillars;

2 She has prepared her food, she has mixed her wine;
   She has also set her table;

3 She has sent out her maidens, she calls
   From the tops of the heights of the city:

4 "Whoever is naive, let him turn in here!"
   To him who lacks understanding she says,

5 "Come, eat of my food
   And drink of the wine I have mixed.

6 "Forsake *your* folly and live,
   And proceed in the way of understanding."

7 He who corrects a scoffer gets dishonor for himself,
   And he who reproves a wicked man *gets* insults for himself.

8 Do not reprove a scoffer, or he will hate you,
   Reprove a wise man and he will love you.

9 Give *instruction* to a wise man and he will be still wiser,
   Teach a righteous man and he will increase *his* learning.

10 The fear of the LORD is the beginning of wisdom,
   And the knowledge of the Holy One is understanding.

11 For by me your days will be multiplied,
   And years of life will be added to you.

12 If you are wise, you are wise for yourself,
   And if you scoff, you alone will bear it.

13 The woman of folly is boisterous,
   She is naive and knows nothing.

14 She sits at the doorway of her house,
   On a seat by the high places of the city,

15 Calling to those who pass by,
   Who are making their paths straight:

16 "Whoever is naive, let him turn in here,"
   And to him who lacks understanding she says,

17 "Stolen water is sweet;
   And bread *eaten* in secret is pleasant."

18 But he does not know that the dead are there,
   That her guests are in the depths of Sheol.

Discuss with your **GROUP** or **PONDER** on your own . . .

What has wisdom done according to Proverbs 9:1-3?

What message does she send out and to whom?

What is the proper response to her? What is the hope?

a Closer Look

READ Proverbs 9:7-10 and **MARK** references to the *wise man* and the *scoffer*. With both also mark the corresponding pronouns.

Proverbs 9:7-10

7   He who corrects a scoffer gets dishonor for himself,
    And he who reproves a wicked man *gets* insults for himself.

8   Do not reprove a scoffer, or he will hate you,
    Reprove a wise man and he will love you.

9   Give *instruction* to a wise man and he will be still wiser,
    Teach a righteous man and he will increase *his* learning.

10 The fear of the LORD is the beginning of wisdom,
    And the knowledge of the Holy One is understanding.

Discuss with your GROUP or PONDER on your own . . .

How does the tone of verses 7-10 differ from those that precede?

ONE STEP FURTHER:

Word Study: Scoffer
Take some time this week to investigate what a scoffer is. Check Proverbs, the rest of the wisdom literature, and then the rest of the Old Testament. Record below what you learn, making sure to address how being a scoffer compares with simply being naive.

ONE STEP FURTHER:

Psalm 1

Take some time to read and meditate on Psalm 1. Record your observations below.

What is the difference in approach?

How is the scoffer of 7-12 different from the naive person of 1-6?

What can you expect if you go toe-to-toe with a scoffer?

What does the response to correction and reproof say about a person? What does your response to correction and reproof say about you?

What happens when you try to invest in a scoffer? Been there? Done that? How did it go?

What happens when you invest in the wise?

What kind of an investment are you? Explain?

What kind of investor have you been? Can you recall a time when you made an investment in someone else that paid dividends? Explain.

What do we learn about the fear of the LORD in Proverbs 9:10?

Describe the woman of folly in verses 13-18.

How does she compare with wisdom (verses 1-6)?

What same phrase do the two call out?

A THOUGHT FROM: *Jan*

Let's Talk About Fools

When you walk through Proverbs, it's amazing to see all God has to say about fools. He talks about the wise as well, but it's the fools that make us sit up and listen. I think this is true because as believers we don't talk about fools. It just doesn't seem very loving; and yet, they would not be so prominent in Proverbs if understanding who they are were not critical to our walk.

When you deal with someone who *always* thinks he is right, who uses anger to control and who trusts in his own heart, you've encountered a fool. Note the word *always*. We all can be foolish at times, but a bona fide fool *always* thinks he's right, *always* uses anger to get his way, and *always* trusts in his own heart; and we need to understand how to deal with him. God doesn't leave us at the mercy of a fool's behavior. If you follow His instructions, you see He is very clear about the folly of trying to reason with a fool. If you have a difficult relationship that leaves you stymied, even though you have tried everything you know to do, it may be you are dealing with a biblical fool. This would be a good time to search the ancient Scriptures for answers. You'll be amazed at how clear God is about how to handle your difficult relationship.

Savvy

GOD'S TRUTH FOR A LIFE THAT WORKS

Fool-Proofing

Still trying to figure out how to deal with scoffers and fools? Jan Silvious unpacks it all in *Fool-Proofing Your Life: How to Deal Effectively with the Impossible People in Your Life.*

How does folly's message differ from wisdom's message? Where does her path lead?

@THE END OF THE DAY . . .

Think back through Proverbs 7, 8, and 9 and consider what you've learned. Then, write one-sentence summaries describing each and give each a hashtag "name" that will help you to easily recall the content. Finally, pray and ask God to impress on you the truths from Proverbs that you most need to focus on this coming week and write them down.

Proverbs 7

One-Sentence Summary

Proverbs 8

One-Sentence Summary

Proverbs 9

One-Sentence Summary

This is the specific truth I'm going to focus on this week:

The Proverbs of Solomon

The proverbs of Solomon.
A wise son makes a father glad,
But a foolish son is a grief to his mother.
–Proverbs 10:1

Feeling confused about work, money, relationships, borrowing, lending, speaking, counsel, animal care, diligence, discipline, inheritances, or anything else? Proverbs probably has something to say to *your* situation! The early chapters of the book speak more to the general concept of wisdom and moral living in longer sections of text. However, beginning in Proverbs 10 we see a shift to stand-alone proverbs. We'll read our texts this week in bigger chunks and return to examine select specifics.

One other thing. We're covering quite a few proverbs this week! For convenience sake they're all included in the lesson. Realize, though, that this makes the lesson *look longer* than it actually is. Breathe. Let's get started!

A THOUGHT FROM:

Road Trip!

The year that our youngest went to college, my husband and I decided to get out of town for a bit to adjust to our new semi-empty nest status. We packed up the Chevy Cruze and set off from the Chicago suburbs on a 34-hour round-trip drive-time to Massachusetts.

What do you do when you're trapped in a car for 34+ hours?

There was a time I was able read in a car, but these days reading is not always a wise car choice. There was a time I could work on my computer, but alas, battery life has become an issue for my elderly MacBook Pro. Of course, the hubby and I did spend quite a few hours talking and solving the problems of the world, but we still had some time on our hands . . . so we listened to Proverbs.

I'm not quite sure how many times we actually made it through because we do like to talk, but if we had been playing the silent game, we would have listened to it 17 times just on the road because it takes just north of 2 hours to listen to the whole thing!

When you're thinking in "drive times," 2 hours is no time at all!

What drive times can you redeem with Proverbs? What other 2-hour time blocks could you use more wisely? Not really a rhetorical question. Go ahead and jot down some ideas below.

Review PROVERBS 1–9

Take a few minutes to think back over what we've studied so far. Be sure to include both *what you've been learning* and *how you've been applying* what you've learned.

Proverbs 1–6

Proverbs 7

Proverbs 8

Proverbs 9

My most important takeaway so far:

A SHIFT IN APPROACH

The proverbs beginning in chapter 10 glisten like co-mingled exotic gems. No chapter is devoted to a single subject which makes it difficult to pick and choose! Topics are swirled together. Think you've gotten past all the "money" proverbs? Think you've taken enough hits on "diligence"? You'll be wrong. The proverbs on pertinent topics keep coming like the tides.

As we study this week, we're going to read Proverbs 10–14 and then Proverbs 15–17 before going back to examine a number of sections more closely. We'll go one step at a time to overview this next robust section of the text. I'm praying that you'll love it as much as I've come to. If you're pressed for time, listen to it on an audio Bible!

GOD'S TRUTH FOR A LIFE THAT WORKS

Observe Proverbs 10

READ Proverbs 10–14. Questions follow the text on page 87.

Proverbs 10

1 The proverbs of Solomon.
  A wise son makes a father glad,
  But a foolish son is a grief to his mother.

2 Ill-gotten gains do not profit,
  But righteousness delivers from death.

3 The LORD will not allow the righteous to hunger,
  But He will reject the craving of the wicked.

4 Poor is he who works with a negligent hand,
  But the hand of the diligent makes rich.

5 He who gathers in summer is a son who acts wisely,
  But he who sleeps in harvest is a son who acts shamefully.

6 Blessings are on the head of the righteous,
  But the mouth of the wicked conceals violence.

7 The memory of the righteous is blessed,
  But the name of the wicked will rot.

8 The wise of heart will receive commands,
  But a babbling fool will be ruined.

9 He who walks in integrity walks securely,
  But he who perverts his ways will be found out.

10 He who winks the eye causes trouble,
  And a babbling fool will be ruined.

11 The mouth of the righteous is a fountain of life,
  But the mouth of the wicked conceals violence.

12 Hatred stirs up strife,
  But love covers all transgressions.

13 On the lips of the discerning, wisdom is found,
  But a rod is for the back of him who lacks understanding.

14 Wise men store up knowledge,
  But with the mouth of the foolish, ruin is at hand.

15 The rich man's wealth is his fortress,
  The ruin of the poor is their poverty.

16 The wages of the righteous is life,
  The income of the wicked, punishment.

17 He is *on* the path of life who heeds instruction,
  But he who ignores reproof goes astray.

18 He who conceals hatred *has* lying lips,
  And he who spreads slander is a fool.

19 When there are many words, transgression is unavoidable,
  But he who restrains his lips is wise.

20 The tongue of the righteous is *as* choice silver,
  The heart of the wicked is *worth* little.

21 The lips of the righteous feed many,
  But fools die for lack of understanding.

22 It is the blessing of the LORD that makes rich,
  And He adds no sorrow to it.

23 Doing wickedness is like sport to a fool,

ONE STEP FURTHER:

The Righteous
If you have extra time this week, read Proverbs 10–14 one more time and list everything you learn about "the righteous."

And *so is* wisdom to a man of understanding.

24 What the wicked fears will come upon him,

But the desire of the righteous will be granted.

25 When the whirlwind passes, the wicked is no more,

But the righteous *has* an everlasting foundation.

26 Like vinegar to the teeth and smoke to the eyes,

So is the lazy one to those who send him.

27 The fear of the LORD prolongs life,

But the years of the wicked will be shortened.

28 The hope of the righteous is gladness,

But the expectation of the wicked perishes.

29 The way of the LORD is a stronghold to the upright,

But ruin to the workers of iniquity.

30 The righteous will never be shaken,

But the wicked will not dwell in the land.

31 The mouth of the righteous flows with wisdom,

But the perverted tongue will be cut out.

32 The lips of the righteous bring forth what is acceptable,

But the mouth of the wicked what is perverted.

Proverbs 11

1 A false balance is an abomination to the LORD,

But a just weight is His delight.

2 When pride comes, then comes dishonor,

But with the humble is wisdom.

3 The integrity of the upright will guide them,

But the crookedness of the treacherous will destroy them.

4 Riches do not profit in the day of wrath,

But righteousness delivers from death.

5 The righteousness of the blameless will smooth his way,

But the wicked will fall by his own wickedness.

6 The righteousness of the upright will deliver them,

But the treacherous will be caught by *their own* greed.

7 When a wicked man dies, *his* expectation will perish,

And the hope of strong men perishes.

8 The righteous is delivered from trouble,

But the wicked takes his place.

9 With *his* mouth the godless man destroys his neighbor,

But through knowledge the righteous will be delivered.

10 When it goes well with the righteous, the city rejoices,

And when the wicked perish, there is joyful shouting.

11 By the blessing of the upright a city is exalted,

But by the mouth of the wicked it is torn down.

12 He who despises his neighbor lacks sense,

But a man of understanding keeps silent.

13 He who goes about as a talebearer reveals secrets,

But he who is trustworthy conceals a matter.

14 Where there is no guidance the people fall,

But in abundance of counselors there is victory.

15 He who is guarantor for a stranger will surely suffer for it,

But he who hates being a guarantor is secure.

16 A gracious woman attains honor,

And ruthless men attain riches.

17 The merciful man does himself good,

But the cruel man does himself harm.

18 The wicked earns deceptive wages,

But he who sows righteousness *gets* a true reward.

19 He who is steadfast in righteousness *will attain* to life,

And he who pursues evil *will bring about* his own death.

20 The perverse in heart are an abomination to the LORD,

But the blameless in *their* walk are His delight.

21 Assuredly, the evil man will not go unpunished,

But the descendants of the righteous will be delivered.

22 *As* a ring of gold in a swine's snout

So is a beautiful woman who lacks discretion.

23 The desire of the righteous is only good,

But the expectation of the wicked is wrath.

24 There is one who scatters, and *yet* increases all the more,

And there is one who withholds what is justly due, *and yet it results* only in want.

25 The generous man will be prosperous,

And he who waters will himself be watered.

26 He who withholds grain, the people will curse him,

But blessing will be on the head of him who sells *it.*

27 He who diligently seeks good seeks favor,

But he who seeks evil, evil will come to him.

28 He who trusts in his riches will fall,

But the righteous will flourish like the *green* leaf.

29 He who troubles his own house will inherit wind,

And the foolish will be servant to the wisehearted.

30 The fruit of the righteous is a tree of life,

And he who is wise wins souls.

31 If the righteous will be rewarded in the earth,

How much more the wicked and the sinner!

Proverbs 12

1 Whoever loves discipline loves knowledge,

But he who hates reproof is stupid.

2 A good man will obtain favor from the LORD,

But He will condemn a man who devises evil.

3 A man will not be established by wickedness,

But the root of the righteous will not be moved.

4 An excellent wife is the crown of her husband,

But she who shames *him* is like rottenness in his bones.

5 The thoughts of the righteous are just,

But the counsels of the wicked are deceitful.

6 The words of the wicked lie in wait for blood,

But the mouth of the upright will deliver them.

7 The wicked are overthrown and are no more,

But the house of the righteous will stand.

Savvy
GOD'S TRUTH FOR A LIFE THAT WORKS

8 A man will be praised according to his insight,

But one of perverse mind will be despised.

9 Better is he who is lightly esteemed and has a servant

Than he who honors himself and lacks bread.

10 A righteous man has regard for the life of his animal,

But *even* the compassion of the wicked is cruel.

11 He who tills his land will have plenty of bread,

But he who pursues worthless *things* lacks sense.

12 The wicked man desires the booty of evil men,

But the root of the righteous yields *fruit*.

13 An evil man is ensnared by the transgression of his lips,

But the righteous will escape from trouble.

14 A man will be satisfied with good by the fruit of his words,

And the deeds of a man's hands will return to him.

15 The way of a fool is right in his own eyes,

But a wise man is he who listens to counsel.

16 A fool's anger is known at once,

But a prudent man conceals dishonor.

17 He who speaks truth tells what is right,

But a false witness, deceit.

18 There is one who speaks rashly like the thrusts of a sword,

But the tongue of the wise brings healing.

19 Truthful lips will be established forever,

But a lying tongue is only for a moment.

20 Deceit is in the heart of those who devise evil,

But counselors of peace have joy.

21 No harm befalls the righteous,

But the wicked are filled with trouble.

22 Lying lips are an abomination to the LORD,

But those who deal faithfully are His delight.

23 A prudent man conceals knowledge,

But the heart of fools proclaims folly.

24 The hand of the diligent will rule,

But the slack *hand* will be put to forced labor.

25 Anxiety in a man's heart weighs it down,

But a good word makes it glad.

26 The righteous is a guide to his neighbor,

But the way of the wicked leads them astray.

27 A lazy man does not roast his prey,

But the precious possession of a man *is* diligence.

28 In the way of righteousness is life,

And in *its* pathway there is no death.

Proverbs 13

1 A wise son *accepts his* father's discipline,

But a scoffer does not listen to rebuke.

2 From the fruit of a man's mouth he enjoys good,

But the desire of the treacherous is violence.

3 The one who guards his mouth preserves his life;

The one who opens wide his lips comes to ruin.

4 The soul of the sluggard craves and *gets* nothing,

But the soul of the diligent is made fat.

5 A righteous man hates falsehood,

But a wicked man acts disgustingly and shamefully.

6 Righteousness guards the one whose way is blameless,

But wickedness subverts the sinner.

7 There is one who pretends to be rich, but has nothing;

Another pretends to be poor, but has great wealth.

8 The ransom of a man's life is his wealth,

But the poor hears no rebuke.

9 The light of the righteous rejoices,

But the lamp of the wicked goes out.

10 Through insolence comes nothing but strife,

But wisdom is with those who receive counsel.

11 Wealth *obtained* by fraud dwindles,

But the one who gathers by labor increases *it*.

12 Hope deferred makes the heart sick,

But desire fulfilled is a tree of life.

13 The one who despises the word will be in debt to it,

But the one who fears the commandment will be rewarded.

14 The teaching of the wise is a fountain of life,

To turn aside from the snares of death.

15 Good understanding produces favor,

16 Every prudent man acts with knowledge,

But a fool displays folly.

17 A wicked messenger falls into adversity,

But a faithful envoy *brings* healing.

18 Poverty and shame *will come* to him who neglects discipline,

But he who regards reproof will be honored.

19 Desire realized is sweet to the soul,

But it is an abomination to fools to turn away from evil.

20 He who walks with wise men will be wise,

But the companion of fools will suffer harm.

21 Adversity pursues sinners,

But the righteous will be rewarded with prosperity.

22 A good man leaves an inheritance to his children's children,

And the wealth of the sinner is stored up for the righteous.

23 Abundant food *is in* the fallow ground of the poor,

But it is swept away by injustice.

24 He who withholds his rod hates his son,

But he who loves him disciplines him diligently.

25 The righteous has enough to satisfy his appetite,

But the stomach of the wicked is in need.

Proverbs 14

1 The wise woman builds her house,

But the foolish tears it down with her own hands.

2 He who walks in his uprightness fears the LORD,

But the way of the treacherous is hard.

But he who is devious in his ways despises Him.

3 In the mouth of the foolish is a rod for *his* back,

But the lips of the wise will protect them.

Savvy

4   Where no oxen are, the manger is clean,

But much revenue *comes* by the strength of the ox.

5   A trustworthy witness will not lie,

But a false witness utters lies.

6   A scoffer seeks wisdom and *finds* none,

But knowledge is easy to one who has understanding.

7   Leave the presence of a fool,

Or you will not discern words of knowledge.

8   The wisdom of the sensible is to understand his way,

But the foolishness of fools is deceit.

9   Fools mock at sin,

But among the upright there is good will.

10   The heart knows its own bitterness,

And a stranger does not share its joy.

11   The house of the wicked will be destroyed,

But the tent of the upright will flourish.

12   There is a way *which seems* right to a man,

But its end is the way of death.

13   Even in laughter the heart may be in pain,

And the end of joy may be grief.

14   The backslider in heart will have his fill of his own ways,

But a good man will *be satisfied* with his.

15   The naive believes everything,

But the sensible man considers his steps.

16   A wise man is cautious and turns away from evil,

But a fool is arrogant and careless.

17   A quick-tempered man acts foolishly,

And a man of evil devices is hated.

18   The naive inherit foolishness,

But the sensible are crowned with knowledge.

19   The evil will bow down before the good,

And the wicked at the gates of the righteous.

20   The poor is hated even by his neighbor,

But those who love the rich are many.

21   He who despises his neighbor sins,

But happy is he who is gracious to the poor.

22   Will they not go astray who devise evil?

But kindness and truth *will be to* those who devise good.

23   In all labor there is profit,

But mere talk *leads* only to poverty.

24   The crown of the wise is their riches,

But the folly of fools is foolishness.

25   A truthful witness saves lives,

But he who utters lies is treacherous.

26   In the fear of the LORD there is strong confidence,

And his children will have refuge.

27   The fear of the LORD is a fountain of life,

That one may avoid the snares of death.

28   In a multitude of people is a king's glory,

But in the dearth of people is a prince's ruin.

29   He who is slow to anger has great understanding,

But he who is quick-tempered exalts folly.

30   A tranquil heart is life to the body,

FYI:

My Favorites

If you're looking for a great audio Bible, my favorites are *The Bible Experience* and *The Word of Promise.*

With both, you can purchase the whole Bible or you can buy it book by book. Might not be a bad idea to buy the Proverbs!

Looking for a free version? Check out www.faithcomesbyhearing.com. You'll find over 500 free audio Bibles in almost every language imaginable!

Savvy

GOD'S TRUTH FOR A LIFE THAT WORKS

But passion is rottenness to the bones.

31 He who oppresses the poor taunts his Maker,

But he who is gracious to the needy honors Him.

32 The wicked is thrust down by his wrongdoing,

But the righteous has a refuge when he dies.

33 Wisdom rests in the heart of one who has understanding,

But in the hearts of fools it is made known.

34 Righteousness exalts a nation,

But sin is a disgrace to *any* people.

35 The king's favor is toward a servant who acts wisely,

But his anger is toward him who acts shamefully.

Discuss with your GROUP or PONDER on your own . . .

What general observations did you make in these chapters? Be concise.

What questions do you have after reading the texts? (Remember, learning to ask good questions is foundational to effective Bible study.)

A THOUGHT FROM:  *Pam*

Remember "Reproof"?

As I read this section of the Proverbs, I find myself reproved more often than I would like. It's not pleasant. When we're reproved, we know there is something in our lives that needs correction.

Maybe you're experiencing the same thing. Maybe you're thinking, "I wish the money proverbs would stop!" or "Will we ever be done with these anger proverbs?" I want to encourage you with words we have already been studying, words from Proverbs 3:11-12: ". . . do not reject the discipline of the LORD or loathe His reproof, for whom the LORD loves He reproves, even as a father *corrects* the son in whom he delights."

Proverbs give us practical insight on righteous living that can be fully realized only by submitting to the work of the Holy Spirit in our lives. Let's not fight Him!

Savvy
GOD'S TRUTH FOR A LIFE THAT WORKS

ONE STEP FURTHER:

Word Study: Righteous

Take some time this week to find the Hebrew word for "righteous." Explore how it is used throughout Proverbs and elsewhere in the Old Testament. Record your findings below.

a Closer Look

READ Proverbs 10–14 again. This time **LIST** the **contrasts/comparisons** you see by general category. I'll get you started.

CONTRASTS

Wise Life	Foolish Death

Do the specific contrasts fit into larger more general categories? If so, how? Why does this matter?

Read Proverbs 10–14 once more. This time **MARK** key, repeated words that you notice, title each chapter, and identify the most applicable verse for you in each.

PROVERBS 10: My Verse(s):

PROVERBS 11: My Verse(s):

PROVERBS 12: My Verse(s):

PROVERBS 13: My Verse(s):

PROVERBS 14: My Verse(s):

PROVERBS 10

Proverbs 10 focuses on *righteousness* with the Hebrew root (*sdq*) appearing thirteen times. It will continue to be a key word in Proverbs 11–13 though not as prevalently. If you didn't mark the words *righteous/righteousness* in Proverbs 10, go back and do it now. Then we'll look more closely at one of the beautiful ways righteousness displays itself.

Read Proverbs 10:19-21 and **MARK** everything related to speaking or words.

Proverbs 10:19-21

19　When there are many words, transgression is unavoidable,
　　But he who restrains his lips is wise.

20　The tongue of the righteous is *as* choice silver,
　　The heart of the wicked is *worth* little.

21　The lips of the righteous feed many,
　　But fools die for lack of understanding.

Discuss with your **GROUP** or **PONDER** on your own . . .

What is "unavoidable" with many words? Why do you think this is?

What do the wise do? How would you rate yourself using this metric for wisdom? Why?

A THOUGHT FROM:

Disengage

How do you solve a problem, say, with a difficult person who always thinks they're right? My natural tendency is almost always to engage and use words, many words, as many words as I can muster to set the person straight!

One of the curious lessons that I've had to learn from Proverbs is that often wisdom disengages. It shuts up and leans back rather than speaking up and leaning in.

Certainly the wise speak, but more often than you'd think, wise people restrain their lips! It's a sobering (and difficult!) thought for those of us who like to talk!

How do you think others would rate you? (Sorry, had to ask.) As you answer, think beyond just the spoken word.

What is the tongue of the righteous like? What do the lips of the righteous do? How does this compare with the "many words" of verse 19?

According to verse 21, why do fools die? How can the righteous help?

How would you recognize a "righteous tongue" in your world? Can you think of any examples among people you know?

PROVERBS 11

 Proverbs 11:4-8 and **MARK** *righteousness, deliver,* and *death.*

Proverbs 11:4-8

4   Riches do not profit in the day of wrath,
    But righteousness delivers from death.

5   The righteousness of the blameless will smooth his way,
    But the wicked will fall by his own wickedness.

6   The righteousness of the upright will deliver them,
    But the treacherous will be caught by *their own* greed.

7   When a wicked man dies, *his* expectation will perish,
    And the hope of strong men perishes.

8   The righteous is delivered from trouble,
    But the wicked takes his place.

True Riches

"Do not store up for yourselves treasures on earth, where moth and rust destroy, and where thieves break in and steal. But store up for yourselves treasures in heaven, where neither moth nor rust destroys, and where thieves do not break in or steal; for where your treasure is, there your heart will be also."

—Jesus, Matthew 6:19-21

GOD'S TRUTH FOR A LIFE THAT WORKS

Discuss with your GROUP or PONDER on your own . . .

When are riches worthless? Why? What will greed do to the treacherous?

What delivers from death?

What does this section teach about righteousness and the righteous?

What hope is there in the face of death if no man is righteous? How is this foundational to the Gospel message?

Righteousness and the Gospel

The Only Way to True Righteousness

If righteousness delivers from death, then righteousness is all important. Take some time to examine the following verses to learn what the Bible teaches about righteousness, death, and life.

Matthew 5:20

Romans 3:9-18

A THOUGHT FROM: *Pam*

Don't Miss This!

By now you probably know I'm all about flexibility. Still, I'm going to highly recommend that if you're flexing this week, you don't flex over this section! Study for yourself about **Righteousness and the Gospel**—it's a matter of life and death!

Savvy

GOD'S TRUTH FOR A LIFE THAT WORKS

A THOUGHT FROM: *Pam*

Just have to vent?

For some reason, "venting" (aka "ranting") on social media has become an accepted form of self-therapy. It's a way to "get it off my chest" without vomiting on someone firsthand. Sometimes it's passive aggressive. We don't call someone out but we sure hope they "just happen" to read our post.

In the estimation of Proverbs, there's a word for that kind of behavior: foolish. While I don't have Proverbs 12:16 taped to the top of my computer, God has written it on my heart . . . but it's been a battle!

Bottom line: If you're angry, pause before you post and read Proverbs 12:16.

FYI:

Matthew 5:13-16

"You are the salt of the earth; but if the salt has become tasteless, how can it be made salty again? It is no longer good for anything, except to be thrown out and trampled under foot by men. You are the light of the world. A city set on a hill cannot be hidden; nor does anyone light a lamp and put it under a basket, but on the lampstand, and it gives light to all who are in the house. Let your light shine before men in such a way that they may see your good works, and glorify your Father who is in heaven."

–Jesus, Matthew 5:13-16

GOD'S TRUTH FOR A LIFE THAT WORKS

Romans 4:1-5

What is the only way people can obtain righteousness that saves?

PROVERBS 12

Read Proverbs 12:15-19, 25 and **MARK** all mouth/speaking related words and all occurrences of *fool* (include synonyms).

Proverbs 12:15-19, 25

15   The way of a fool is right in his own eyes,

But a wise man is he who listens to counsel.

16   A fool's anger is known at once,

But a prudent man conceals dishonor.

17   He who speaks truth tells what is right,

But a false witness, deceit.

18   There is one who speaks rashly like the thrusts of a sword,

But the tongue of the wise brings healing.

19   Truthful lips will be established forever,

But a lying tongue is only for a moment.

25   Anxiety in a man's heart weighs it down,

But a good word makes it glad.

Discuss with your GROUP or PONDER on your own . . .

Describe the fool in verses 15-16. How do the wise contrast? What characterizes them?

What positive "speaking" words did you note? How can you use your mouth for good? What effect will it have?

What can help an anxious heart? How are you doing at helping the anxious hearts of others? How have others ministered to you?

PROVERBS 13

Read Proverbs 13:20 and **MARK** the word *wise*.

Proverbs 13:20

20 He who walks with wise men will be wise,

But the companion of fools will suffer harm.

Discuss with your **GROUP** or **PONDER** on your own . . .

What effect will your companions have on you?

Are you a good person to walk with? Why/why not?

How does being salt and light relate to this proverb?

A THOUGHT FROM: *Pam*

Who are you walking with?

Although I'm a writer, I lack words to describe the depth of influence wise people have had on my life and how profoundly God has used them to shape me. Some I had nothing to do with—I was born into a family that loves and follows God wholeheartedly. My parents live so wisely and with such love that most of my friends wanted them as their parents (they still do!)—seriously, they verbalize this—and now my kids' friends want them as their grandparents. I see my parents in the pages of Proverbs in the way they speak and share and live. It was a gift to grow up in their home and it is a gift to still live close by them today. If I'm half the person that they are, I will have lived well.

Perhaps because I've been surrounded by wisdom from birth, I've been compelled to seek it out. Some of the wise I've walked with have been peers who have spurred me on to follow hard after Jesus. Others have been mentors whom I have pursued so I can learn from their lives and from their walk with the Lord without having to repeat mistakes and missteps.

A critical piece of walking with the wise for me today is my small group. We meet every Sunday night and we talk through the Word which we've all been studying the previous week. These are disciples of Jesus, brothers and sisters in Christ who encourage me in God and who spur me on to love and good deeds!

Who are you walking with?

Savvy

GOD'S TRUTH FOR A LIFE THAT WORKS

FYI:

Psalm 119:130

The unfolding of Your words gives light;

It gives understanding to the simple.

ONE STEP FURTHER:

Listen, yes! Believe all, no!

One of the most promising figures among the kings of Judah was a child king named Joash. Saved from his murderous, crown-seeking grandmother, Joash lived because Jehoiada—who was both a priest and his uncle—saved him. The boy Joash did well for much of his life because he listened to Jehoiada. When Jehoiada died, though, King Joash kept listening but with grave results when he listened to wrong voices.

If you have time this week, read the account of King Joash and Jehoiada in 2 Chronicles 24 and 2 Kings 11–12. Record your observations below and consider how Joash could have benefited from Proverbs 14:15-18.

What practical steps can you take to walk with others who are wiser than you?

What about investing in others who could benefit by walking with you?

PROVERBS 14

Read Proverbs 14:15-18 and **MARK** *naive* and *sensible.*

Proverbs 14:15-18

15 The naive believes everything,

But the sensible man considers his steps.

16 A wise man is cautious and turns away from evil,

But a fool is arrogant and careless.

17 A quick-tempered man acts foolishly,

And a man of evil devices is hated.

18 The naive inherit foolishness,

But the sensible are crowned with knowledge.

Discuss with your **GROUP** or **PONDER** on your own . . .

How does the sensible man of verse 15 differ from the naive?

What is the inherent danger in believing everything?

Savvy

GOD'S TRUTH FOR A LIFE THAT WORKS

Do you think Christians are more susceptible to believe-everything behaviors? Why/ why not? What about you?

How do the wise and sensible live?

What wisdom from these proverbs can you apply to specific situations today?

Observe Proverbs 15-17

READ Proverbs 15–17. Questions will follow on page 99.

Proverbs 15

1 A gentle answer turns away wrath,

But a harsh word stirs up anger.

2 The tongue of the wise makes knowledge acceptable,

But the mouth of fools spouts folly.

3 The eyes of the LORD are in every place,

Watching the evil and the good.

4 A soothing tongue is a tree of life,

But perversion in it crushes the spirit.

5 A fool rejects his father's discipline,

But he who regards reproof is sensible.

6 Great wealth is *in* the house of the righteous,

But trouble is in the income of the wicked.

7 The lips of the wise spread knowledge,

But the hearts of fools are not so.

8 The sacrifice of the wicked is an abomination to the LORD,

But the prayer of the upright is His delight.

9 The way of the wicked is an abomination to the LORD,

But He loves one who pursues righteousness.

10 Grievous punishment is for him who forsakes the way;

He who hates reproof will die.

11 Sheol and Abaddon *lie open* before the LORD,

How much more the hearts of men!

12 A scoffer does not love one who reproves him,

He will not go to the wise.

A THOUGHT FROM: *Pam*

Hook. Line. Sinker.

I remember when I used to believe everything. Look into my eyes, tell me your sad story, and any cash that I had would be yours. I remember one time specifically where I was most certainly fleeced. I was in Chattanooga for a huge women's conference. While walking to my car after dinner with my new best friends from the conference, a woman approached us with a sad story about needing gas for her car that was broken down on the highway. There was some other urgency to the story that I've repressed over the years, but bottom line: I bit. Hook. Line. Sinker.

Fortunately I was carrying only $40. One of the wiser women in the group politely declined and later told me I'd been had. She knew the game. She saw the holes in the story. Why was this woman asking for money near a row of restaurants when her car was supposedly on the highway miles away? In retrospect I realized I'd just learned a $40 lesson. My wise friend, Jan Silvious, often says that an education is expensive and you pay for it in many different ways. Lesson learned.

I was naive (Hebrew: *pethiy*) but I've learned. If you're feeling naive, realize there is hope! Remember, one of the reasons Proverbs was written and compiled was "To give prudence to the naive" (Proverbs 1:4).

FYI:

Psalm 19:7b
The testimony of the LORD is sure, making wise the simple.

Savvy

GOD'S TRUTH FOR A LIFE THAT WORKS

13 A joyful heart makes a cheerful face,

But when the heart is sad, the spirit is broken.

14 The mind of the intelligent seeks knowledge,

But the mouth of fools feeds on folly.

15 All the days of the afflicted are bad,

But a cheerful heart *has* a continual feast.

16 Better is a little with the fear of the LORD

Than great treasure and turmoil with it.

17 Better is a dish of vegetables where love is

Than a fattened ox *served* with hatred.

18 A hot-tempered man stirs up strife,

But the slow to anger calms a dispute.

19 The way of the lazy is as a hedge of thorns,

But the path of the upright is a highway.

20 A wise son makes a father glad,

But a foolish man despises his mother.

21 Folly is joy to him who lacks sense,

But a man of understanding walks straight.

22 Without consultation, plans are frustrated,

But with many counselors they succeed.

23 A man has joy in an apt answer,

And how delightful is a timely word!

24 The path of life *leads* upward for the wise

That he may keep away from Sheol below.

25 The LORD will tear down the house of the proud,

But He will establish the boundary of the widow.

26 Evil plans are an abomination to the LORD,

But pleasant words are pure.

27 He who profits illicitly troubles his own house,

But he who hates bribes will live.

28 The heart of the righteous ponders how to answer,

But the mouth of the wicked pours out evil things.

29 The LORD is far from the wicked,

But He hears the prayer of the righteous.

30 Bright eyes gladden the heart;

Good news puts fat on the bones.

31 He whose ear listens to the life-giving reproof

Will dwell among the wise.

32 He who neglects discipline despises himself,

But he who listens to reproof acquires understanding.

33 The fear of the LORD is the instruction for wisdom,

And before honor *comes* humility.

Proverbs 16

1 The plans of the heart belong to man,

But the answer of the tongue is from the LORD.

2 All the ways of a man are clean in his own sight,

But the LORD weighs the motives.

3 Commit your works to the LORD

And your plans will be established.

4 The LORD has made everything for its own purpose,

Even the wicked for the day of evil.

5 Everyone who is proud in heart is an abomination to the LORD;

Assuredly, he will not be unpunished.

6 By lovingkindness and truth iniquity is atoned for,

And by the fear of the LORD one keeps away from evil.

7 When a man's ways are pleasing to the LORD,

He makes even his enemies to be at peace with him.

8 Better is a little with righteousness

Than great income with injustice.

9 The mind of man plans his way,

But the LORD directs his steps.

10 A divine decision is in the lips of the king;

His mouth should not err in judgment.

11 A just balance and scales belong to the LORD;

All the weights of the bag are His concern.

12 It is an abomination for kings to commit wicked acts,

For a throne is established on righteousness.

13 Righteous lips are the delight of kings,

And he who speaks right is loved.

14 The fury of a king is *like* messengers of death,

But a wise man will appease it.

15 In the light of a king's face is life,

And his favor is like a cloud with the spring rain.

16 How much better it is to get wisdom than gold!

And to get understanding is to be chosen above silver.

17 The highway of the upright is to depart from evil;

He who watches his way preserves his life.

18 Pride *goes* before destruction,

And a haughty spirit before stumbling.

19 It is better to be humble in spirit with the lowly

Than to divide the spoil with the proud.

20 He who gives attention to the word will find good,

And blessed is he who trusts in the LORD.

21 The wise in heart will be called understanding,

And sweetness of speech increases persuasiveness.

22 Understanding is a fountain of life to one who has it,

But the discipline of fools is folly.

23 The heart of the wise instructs his mouth

And adds persuasiveness to his lips.

24 Pleasant words are a honeycomb,

Sweet to the soul and healing to the bones.

25 There is a way *which seems* right to a man,

But its end is the way of death.

26 A worker's appetite works for him,

For his hunger urges him *on.*

27 A worthless man digs up evil,

While his words are like scorching fire.

28 A perverse man spreads strife,

And a slanderer separates intimate friends.

29 A man of violence entices his neighbor

And leads him in a way that is not good.

30 He who winks his eyes *does so* to devise perverse things;

He who compresses his lips brings evil to pass.

31 A gray head is a crown of glory;

It is found in the way of righteousness.

Savvy

GOD'S TRUTH FOR A LIFE THAT WORKS

32 He who is slow to anger is better than the mighty,

And he who rules his spirit, than he who captures a city.

33 The lot is cast into the lap,

But its every decision is from the LORD.

Proverbs 17

1 Better is a dry morsel and quietness with it

Than a house full of feasting with strife.

2 A servant who acts wisely will rule over a son who acts shamefully,

And will share in the inheritance among brothers.

3 The refining pot is for silver and the furnace for gold,

But the LORD tests hearts.

4 An evildoer listens to wicked lips;

A liar pays attention to a destructive tongue.

5 He who mocks the poor taunts his Maker;

He who rejoices at calamity will not go unpunished.

6 Grandchildren are the crown of old men,

And the glory of sons is their fathers.

7 Excellent speech is not fitting for a fool,

Much less are lying lips to a prince.

8 A bribe is a charm in the sight of its owner;

Wherever he turns, he prospers.

9 He who conceals a transgression seeks love,

But he who repeats a matter separates intimate friends.

10 A rebuke goes deeper into one who has understanding

Than a hundred blows into a fool.

11 A rebellious man seeks only evil,

So a cruel messenger will be sent against him.

12 Let a man meet a bear robbed of her cubs,

Rather than a fool in his folly.

13 He who returns evil for good,

Evil will not depart from his house.

14 The beginning of strife is *like* letting out water,

So abandon the quarrel before it breaks out.

15 He who justifies the wicked and he who condemns the righteous,

Both of them alike are an abomination to the LORD.

16 Why is there a price in the hand of a fool to buy wisdom,

When he has no sense?

17 A friend loves at all times,

And a brother is born for adversity.

18 A man lacking in sense pledges

And becomes guarantor in the presence of his neighbor.

19 He who loves transgression loves strife;

He who raises his door seeks destruction.

20 He who has a crooked mind finds no good,

And he who is perverted in his language falls into evil.

21 He who sires a fool *does so* to his sorrow,

And the father of a fool has no joy.

22 A joyful heart is good medicine,

But a broken spirit dries up the bones.

23 A wicked man receives a bribe from the bosom

To pervert the ways of justice.

24 Wisdom is in the presence of the one who has understanding,

> But the eyes of a fool are on the ends of the earth.
>
> 25 A foolish son is a grief to his father
>
> And bitterness to her who bore him.
>
> 26 It is also not good to fine the righteous,
>
> *Nor* to strike the noble for *their* uprightness.
>
> 27 He who restrains his words has knowledge,
>
> And he who has a cool spirit is a man of understanding.
>
> 28 Even a fool, when he keeps silent, is considered wise;
>
> When he closes his lips, he is *considered* prudent.

Discuss with your GROUP or PONDER on your own . . .

What general observations did you make in these chapters? Be concise.

What questions do you have after reading the text?

Read Proverbs 15–17 again. This time **LIST** the **contrasts/comparisons** you see by general category. I'll get you started.

CONTRASTS

Wise Life	Foolish Death

ONE STEP FURTHER:

Warning Signs

If you have time this week, read back through Proverbs 15–17 noting warning signs that foolish and wicked people give off. What behaviors characterize them? What dangers can we expect if we allow ourselves to be entangled with them?

Savvy

GOD'S TRUTH FOR A LIFE THAT WORKS

A THOUGHT FROM: *JAN*

Good Words Have Incredible Power

One of the greatest joys of my life is see someone change who has come into my office weighted down with cares that have caused them to have "troubled eyes." Concern, worry and terror have afflicted their mind to the point it has changed their affect. I recognize "the look" of many sorrows, of draining depression and agonizing anxiety. Amazingly I've seen that "look" change in minutes with the news that good words bring.

I have seen clouded eyes clear with the soothing words of God's unfailing love and acceptance. I've seen tense teary eyes relax from heavy cares with the reminder that we can "cast all our care" on Him, and I've seen dull eyes sparkle when Truth washes away false guilt that has weighted down a tender soul.

Words are just letters woven together, but in the right combination they can become swords of destruction or bottles of healing ointment. Isn't it amazing that God has put the skill to kill or to bring life in the same mouth? It's all in our power to decide how we're going to use our words.

When you see "troubled eyes," ask God to give you words that bring life, truth, clarity, healing and love and watch the miracle of change happen right before your eyes.

a Closer Look

READ Proverbs 15–17 one more time. This time **MARK** key, repeated words that you notice, title each chapter, and identify the most applicable verse for you in each.

PROVERBS 15: My Verse(s):

PROVERBS 16: My Verse(s):

PROVERBS 17: My Verse(s):

PROVERBS 15

Read Proverbs 15:1-4 and **MARK** mouth words.

Proverbs 15:1-4

1   A gentle answer turns away wrath,
    But a harsh word stirs up anger.

2   The tongue of the wise makes knowledge acceptable,
    But the mouth of fools spouts folly.

3   The eyes of the LORD are in every place,
    Watching the evil and the good.

4   A soothing tongue is a tree of life,
    But perversion in it crushes the spirit.

Discuss with your GROUP or PONDER on your own . . .

How can words spoken change a situation?

Are you more likely to turn wrath away or stir up anger by inviting it in for a cup of coffee? Explain.

What makes knowledge acceptable? Based on what you've learned about wisdom, why do you think this is?

When you speak, how are *you* at making knowledge acceptable?

PROVERBS 16

Read Proverbs 16:21-25 and **MARK** occurrences of *wise* and *persuasiveness.*

Proverbs 16:21-25

21   The wise in heart will be called understanding,
     And sweetness of speech increases persuasiveness.

22   Understanding is a fountain of life to one who has it,
     But the discipline of fools is folly.

23   The heart of the wise instructs his mouth
     And adds persuasiveness to his lips.

ONE STEP FURTHER:

Soothing Tongues
Reflect for a moment on your life. Who delivers the most gentle answers and speaks with a soothing tongue? How do these people diffuse situations? What can you learn from observing and emulating them?

Savvy
GOD'S TRUTH FOR A LIFE THAT WORKS

24 Pleasant words are a honeycomb,

   Sweet to the soul and healing to the bones.

25 There is a way *which seems* right to a man,

   But its end is the way of death.

Discuss with your GROUP or PONDER on your own . . .

What does Proverbs 16:21 say about the "wise in heart"? What is associated with this?

What relationship does the heart have with the mouth?

What kind of words come from the mouths of wise people according to the text?

What effect does this type of speech have on people?

Why is this so important? Take into consideration Proverbs 16:24 as you answer.

Do you know anyone whose words are "sweet to the soul and healing to the bones"? Describe the circumstances and the effect.

GOD'S TRUTH FOR A LIFE THAT WORKS

How are you in this regard? What do your words "taste" like? Any room for improvement? Just asking.

Digging Deeper

Pick Your Own Topic

Pick a topic—mouth, money, righteousness, foolishness—anything Proverbs talks about repeatedly and look at everything it says. Overachievers can cross-reference the rest of God's Word, too!

PROVERBS 17

Read Proverbs 17:10 and **MARK** *man of understanding* and *fool*.

Proverbs 17:10

10   A rebuke goes deeper into one who has understanding

      Than a hundred blows into a fool.

Discuss with your GROUP or PONDER on your own . . .

How does a man of understanding differ from a fool with regard to correction?

How does this align with the rest of Proverbs?

Does the way you deal with people take this proverb into account? Explain.

@THE END OF THE DAY . . .

This week go into your world with sweetness of speech that heals.

Lesson Seven
Proverbs of Solomon and More!

The name of the LORD is a strong tower; the righteous
runs into it and is safe.
–Proverbs 18:10

As we continue to forage through Proverbs this week, we'll encounter more of Solomon's short sayings up to the middle of chapter 22. After that, the landscape changes a bit as it returns to longer groupings of wise sayings. As we did last week, we'll overview the material and then circle back to look at portions of the text in further depth.

If you're feeling the weight of the text, the breadth and width of righteous living, be encouraged. We learn wisdom over a lifetime, and we walk righteously by the power of the indwelling Holy Spirit. You are not alone!

 PROVERBS 1-17

Take a few minutes to think back over what we've studied so far. Be sure to include what you've learned and how you've applied it.

Proverbs 1–9

Proverbs 10–17

Biggest overall takeaway so far:

Has anything shocked you or made you seriously rethink your thinking, behavior, or speech?

CONTINUING THE PROVERBS OF SOLOMON

As mentioned, Proverbs 18–22:16 continues proverbs attributed to Solomon.

Observe Proverbs 18-22:16

READ Proverbs 18–22:16. Just overview the chapters and enjoy the reading. Questions will follow on page 112.

Proverbs 18

1 He who separates himself seeks *his own* desire,

 He quarrels against all sound wisdom.

2 A fool does not delight in understanding,

 But only in revealing his own mind.

3 When a wicked man comes, contempt also comes,

 And with dishonor *comes* scorn.

4 The words of a man's mouth are deep waters;

 The fountain of wisdom is a bubbling brook.

5 To show partiality to the wicked is not good,

 Nor to thrust aside the righteous in judgment.

6 A fool's lips bring strife,

 And his mouth calls for blows.

7 A fool's mouth is his ruin,

 And his lips are the snare of his soul.

8 The words of a whisperer are like dainty morsels,

 And they go down into the innermost parts of the body.

9 He also who is slack in his work Is brother to him who destroys.

10 The name of the LORD is a strong tower;

 The righteous runs into it and is safe.

11 A rich man's wealth is his strong city,

 And like a high wall in his own imagination.

12 Before destruction the heart of man is haughty,

 But humility *goes* before honor.

13 He who gives an answer before he hears,

 It is folly and shame to him.

14 The spirit of a man can endure his sickness,

 But *as for* a broken spirit who can bear it?

15 The mind of the prudent acquires knowledge,

 And the ear of the wise seeks knowledge.

16 A man's gift makes room for him

 And brings him before great men.

17 The first to plead his case *seems* right,

 Until another comes and examines him.

18 The *cast* lot puts an end to strife

 And decides between the mighty ones.

19 A brother offended *is harder to be won* than a strong city,

 And contentions are like the bars of a citadel.

20 With the fruit of a man's mouth his stomach will be satisfied;

 He will be satisfied *with* the product of his lips.

21 Death and life are in the power of the tongue,

 And those who love it will eat its fruit.

22 He who finds a wife finds a good thing

And obtains favor from the LORD.

23 The poor man utters supplications,

But the rich man answers roughly.

Proverbs 19

1 Better is a poor man who walks in his integrity

Than he who is perverse in speech and is a fool.

2 Also it is not good for a person to be without knowledge,

And he who hurries his footsteps errs.

3 The foolishness of man ruins his way,

And his heart rages against the LORD.

4 Wealth adds many friends,

But a poor man is separated from his friend.

5 A false witness will not go unpunished,

And he who tells lies will not escape.

6 Many will seek the favor of a generous man,

And every man is a friend to him who gives gifts.

7 All the brothers of a poor man hate him;

How much more do his friends abandon him!

He pursues *them with* words, *but* they are gone.

8 He who gets wisdom loves his own soul;

He who keeps understanding will find good.

9 A false witness will not go unpunished,

And he who tells lies will perish.

10 Luxury is not fitting for a fool;

Much less for a slave to rule over princes.

11 A man's discretion makes him slow to anger,

24 A man of *too many* friends *comes* to ruin,

But there is a friend who sticks closer than a brother.

And it is his glory to overlook a transgression.

12 The king's wrath is like the roaring of a lion,

But his favor is like dew on the grass.

13 A foolish son is destruction to his father,

And the contentions of a wife are a constant dripping.

14 House and wealth are an inheritance from fathers,

But a prudent wife is from the LORD.

15 Laziness casts into a deep sleep,

And an idle man will suffer hunger.

16 He who keeps the commandment keeps his soul,

But he who is careless of conduct will die.

17 One who is gracious to a poor man lends to the LORD,

And He will repay him for his good deed.

18 Discipline your son while there is hope,

And do not desire his death.

19 *A man of* great anger will bear the penalty,

For if you rescue *him,* you will only have to do it again.

20 Listen to counsel and accept discipline,

That you may be wise the rest of your days.

21 Many plans are in a man's heart,

But the counsel of the LORD will stand.

22 What is desirable in a man is his kindness,

GOD'S TRUTH FOR A LIFE THAT WORKS

And *it is* better to be a poor man than a liar.

23 The fear of the LORD *leads* to life,

So that one may sleep satisfied, untouched by evil.

24 The sluggard buries his hand in the dish,

But will not even bring it back to his mouth.

25 Strike a scoffer and the naive may become shrewd,

But reprove one who has understanding and he will gain knowledge.

Proverbs 20

1 Wine is a mocker, strong drink a brawler,

And whoever is intoxicated by it is not wise.

2 The terror of a king is like the growling of a lion;

He who provokes him to anger forfeits his own life.

3 Keeping away from strife is an honor for a man,

But any fool will quarrel.

4 The sluggard does not plow after the autumn,

So he begs during the harvest and has nothing.

5 A plan in the heart of a man is *like* deep water,

But a man of understanding draws it out.

6 Many a man proclaims his own loyalty,

But who can find a trustworthy man?

7 A righteous man who walks in his integrity—

How blessed are his sons after him.

8 A king who sits on the throne of justice

Disperses all evil with his eyes.

9 Who can say, "I have cleansed my heart,

I am pure from my sin"?

26 He who assaults *his* father *and* drives *his* mother away

Is a shameful and disgraceful son.

27 Cease listening, my son, to discipline,

And you will stray from the words of knowledge.

28 A rascally witness makes a mockery of justice,

And the mouth of the wicked spreads iniquity.

29 Judgments are prepared for scoffers,

And blows for the back of fools.

10 Differing weights and differing measures,

Both of them are abominable to the LORD.

11 It is by his deeds that a lad distinguishes himself

If his conduct is pure and right.

12 The hearing ear and the seeing eye,

The LORD has made both of them.

13 Do not love sleep, or you will become poor;

Open your eyes, *and* you will be satisfied with food.

14 "Bad, bad," says the buyer,

But when he goes his way, then he boasts.

15 There is gold, and an abundance of jewels;

But the lips of knowledge are a more precious thing.

16 Take his garment when he becomes surety for a stranger;

And for foreigners, hold him in pledge.

17 Bread obtained by falsehood is sweet to a man,

But afterward his mouth will be filled with gravel.

18 Prepare plans by consultation,

And make war by wise guidance.

Savvy

GOD'S TRUTH FOR A LIFE THAT WORKS

19 He who goes about as a slanderer reveals secrets,

Therefore do not associate with a gossip.

20 He who curses his father or his mother,

His lamp will go out in time of darkness.

21 An inheritance gained hurriedly at the beginning

Will not be blessed in the end.

22 Do not say, "I will repay evil";

Wait for the LORD, and He will save you.

23 Differing weights are an abomination to the LORD,

And a false scale is not good.

24 Man's steps are *ordained* by the LORD,

How then can man understand his way?

25 It is a trap for a man to say rashly, "It is holy!"

And after the vows to make inquiry.

26 A wise king winnows the wicked,

And drives the *threshing* wheel over them.

27 The spirit of man is the lamp of the LORD,

Searching all the innermost parts of his being.

28 Loyalty and truth preserve the king,

And he upholds his throne by righteousness.

29 The glory of young men is their strength,

And the honor of old men is their gray hair.

30 Stripes that wound scour away evil,

And strokes *reach* the innermost parts.

Proverbs 21

1 The king's heart is *like* channels of water in the hand of the LORD;

He turns it wherever He wishes.

2 Every man's way is right in his own eyes,

But the LORD weighs the hearts.

3 To do righteousness and justice

Is desired by the LORD more than sacrifice.

4 Haughty eyes and a proud heart,

The lamp of the wicked, is sin.

5 The plans of the diligent *lead* surely to advantage,

But everyone who is hasty *comes* surely to poverty.

6 The acquisition of treasures by a lying tongue

Is a fleeting vapor, the pursuit of death.

7 The violence of the wicked will drag them away,

Because they refuse to act with justice.

8 The way of a guilty man is crooked,

But as for the pure, his conduct is upright.

9 It is better to live in a corner of a roof

Than in a house shared with a contentious woman.

10 The soul of the wicked desires evil;

His neighbor finds no favor in his eyes.

11 When the scoffer is punished, the naive becomes wise;

But when the wise is instructed, he receives knowledge.

12 The righteous one considers the house of the wicked,

Turning the wicked to ruin.

13 He who shuts his ear to the cry of the poor

Will also cry himself and not be answered.

14 A gift in secret subdues anger,

And a bribe in the bosom, strong wrath.

15 The exercise of justice is joy for the righteous,

But is terror to the workers of iniquity.

16 A man who wanders from the way of understanding

Will rest in the assembly of the dead.

17 He who loves pleasure *will become* a poor man;

He who loves wine and oil will not become rich.

18 The wicked is a ransom for the righteous,

And the treacherous is in the place of the upright.

19 It is better to live in a desert land

Than with a contentious and vexing woman.

20 There is precious treasure and oil in the dwelling of the wise,

But a foolish man swallows it up.

21 He who pursues righteousness and loyalty

Finds life, righteousness and honor.

22 A wise man scales the city of the mighty

And brings down the stronghold in which they trust.

23 He who guards his mouth and his tongue,

Guards his soul from troubles.

24 "Proud," "Haughty," "Scoffer," are his names,

Who acts with insolent pride.

25 The desire of the sluggard puts him to death,

For his hands refuse to work;

26 All day long he is craving,

While the righteous gives and does not hold back.

27 The sacrifice of the wicked is an abomination,

How much more when he brings it with evil intent!

28 A false witness will perish,

But the man who listens *to the truth* will speak forever.

29 A wicked man displays a bold face,

But as for the upright, he makes his way sure.

30 There is no wisdom and no understanding

And no counsel against the LORD.

31 The horse is prepared for the day of battle,

But victory belongs to the LORD.

Proverbs 22

1 A *good* name is to be more desired than great wealth,

Favor is better than silver and gold.

2 The rich and the poor have a common bond,

The LORD is the maker of them all.

3 The prudent sees the evil and hides himself,

But the naive go on, and are punished for it.

4 The reward of humility *and* the fear of the LORD

Are riches, honor and life.

5 Thorns *and* snares are in the way of the perverse;

He who guards himself will be far from them.

6 Train up a child in the way he should go,

Even when he is old he will not depart from it.

7 The rich rules over the poor,

And the borrower *becomes* the lender's slave.

8 He who sows iniquity will reap vanity,

Savvy

GOD'S TRUTH FOR A LIFE THAT WORKS

And the rod of his fury will perish.

9 He who is generous will be blessed,
For he gives some of his food to the poor.

10 Drive out the scoffer, and contention will go out,
Even strife and dishonor will cease.

11 He who loves purity of heart
And whose speech is gracious, the king is his friend.

12 The eyes of the LORD preserve knowledge,
But He overthrows the words of the treacherous man.

13 The sluggard says, "There is a lion outside;
I will be killed in the streets!"

14 The mouth of an adulteress is a deep pit;
He who is cursed of the LORD will fall into it.

15 Foolishness is bound up in the heart of a child;
The rod of discipline will remove it far from him.

16 He who oppresses the poor to make more for himself
Or who gives to the rich, *will* only *come to* poverty.

Discuss with your GROUP or PONDER on your own . . .

What general observations did you make in these chapters? Be concise.

INDUCTIVE FOCUS:

Reading and Asking Questions

Remember, the heart of inductive study is slowing down, reading carefully and asking questions. The more you come up with questions on your own, the more equipped you will be to handle accurately the Word of Truth . . . and pass it along to others!

What questions do you have after reading the text?

GOD'S TRUTH FOR A LIFE THAT WORKS

Read Proverbs 18–22:16 again. This time **MARK** key, repeated words that you notice, title each chapter, and identify the most applicable verse or verses for you in each.

PROVERBS 18: My Verse(s):

PROVERBS 19: My Verse(s):

PROVERBS 20: My Verse(s):

PROVERBS 21: My Verse(s):

PROVERBS 22A: My Verse(s):

ONE STEP FURTHER:

The Strong Towers and Cities

If you have some extra time this week, note what Proverbs 18 says about strong towers and cities. How does the strong tower in verse 10 compare with the strong city in verse 11? Which is more stable and why?

How does the usage of "strong city" in Proverbs 18:19 differ from that in verse 11? How can you heed that warning?

Savvy
GOD'S TRUTH FOR A LIFE THAT WORKS

FYI:

The Broken Spirit

The Hebrew word translated "broken" in verse 14 is *nekeah* (broken), from the noun *nakeh*. It carries the idea of beaten, crushed, hopeless.

a Closer Look

PROVERBS 18

Again, the mouth draws attention to itself throughout Proverbs 18, and the reader learns in verse 21 that, indeed, "Death and life are in the power of the tongue." Today let's consider the possible connection between words and a broken spirit.

 Read Proverbs 18:14 and **MARK** the *spirit.*

Proverbs 18:14

14   The spirit of a man can endure his sickness,

But *as for* a broken spirit who can bear it?

Discuss with your GROUP or PONDER on your own . . .

According to this verse, how does physical sickness compare to a broken spirit? Which is worse?

Have you experienced this in your life? Explain.

What types of things can cause a broken spirit?

What effects can our words have on others? Answer both from Proverbs and from your own experience.

Savvy

How can you speak life instead of death? How have others done that for you?

Digging Deeper

"You are lazy, very lazy . . ."

If you have some extra time this week, read through the account of Pharaoh, Moses, and the children of Israel in Exodus 4:27–6:9. In it you'll see how a crushed spirit—in this case literally, "short" [*qotser*] spirit—can cripple not only people but nations.

How do the people respond to the initial good word from God at the end of Exodus 4? What do these good words give them?

What changes in Exodus 5? What does Pharaoh say?

What happens to the peoples' collective spirit?

Do your words give true hope? Do they inflict hurt—intentionally or otherwise?

Proverbs 15:13
A joyful heart makes a cheerful face,
But when the heart is sad, the spirit is broken.

Proverbs 17:22
A joyful heart is good medicine,
But a broken spirit dries up the bones.

The Poor

Proverbs 19:17 says the "One who is gracious to a poor man lends to the LORD . . . ." Certainly that is a call to action. Take some time this week to investigate throughout the pages of Scripture how God's people are to treat those in need. Is there a difference between believers and unbelievers? How are we to discern need? There are so, so many questions to look at! Dive in to see what you can discover and then record your findings below.

PROVERBS 19–20

While earlier chapters linked poverty to slack discipline and negligence, Proverbs 19 commends the poor who walk in integrity. In fact, the word used for "poor" in Proverbs 19:1, 7 and 22 appears four times in the books of 1 and 2 Samuel in accounts relating to David. Let's take a look at those and also consider the role of a king in the nation's life.

 Read Proverbs 19:1, 7, and 22 and **MARK** *poor* and associated pronouns.

Proverbs 19:1, 7, 22

1   Better is a poor man who walks in his integrity
      Than he who is perverse in speech and is a fool.

7   All the brothers of a poor man hate him;
      How much more do his friends abandon him!
      He pursues *them with* words, *but* they are gone.

22   What is desirable in a man is his kindness,
      And *it is* better to be a poor man than a liar.

Discuss with your **GROUP** or **PONDER** on your own . . .

What do these proverbs say about the poor man?

What challenges does he face? Why do you think this is?

How can the "better than" statements of verses 1 and 22 be a helpful reminder during hard times?

Let's Look a Little Closer . . .

The Hebrew word for "poor" (*rush*) in Proverbs 19:1, 7, and 22 is rare outside of Proverbs. Where it does show up, though, is instructive. Let's take a look.

Read 1 Samuel 18:20-25 and **MARK** *poor* and the man who calls himself poor.

1 Samuel 18:20-25

20 Now Michal, Saul's daughter, loved David. When they told Saul, the thing was agreeable to him.

21 Saul thought, "I will give her to him that she may become a snare to him, and that the hand of the Philistines may be against him." Therefore Saul said to David, "For a second time you may be my son-in-law today."

22 Then Saul commanded his servants, "Speak to David secretly, saying, 'Behold, the king delights in you, and all his servants love you; now therefore, become the king's son-in-law.' "

23 So Saul's servants spoke these words to David. But David said, "Is it trivial in your sight to become the king's son-in-law, since I am a poor man and lightly esteemed?"

24 The servants of Saul reported to him according to these words *which* David spoke.

25 Saul then said, "Thus you shall say to David, 'The king does not desire any dowry except a hundred foreskins of the Philistines, to take vengeance on the king's enemies.' " Now Saul planned to make David fall by the hand of the Philistines.

Discuss with your **GROUP** or **PONDER** on your own . . .

Identify and describe the main characters. How are they related to one another? Briefly describe the situation.

How does David describe himself in verse 23? From what you know of Scripture, what was his life like at the time? Was he walking with God? Was he walking in integrity?

Savvy
GOD'S TRUTH FOR A LIFE THAT WORKS

Let's Fast Forward . . .

Years pass between David's odd bridal payment for Michal and the next scene from his life we'll look at. Again, the word "poor" (Hebrew: *rush*) appears in the text, but this time it is not in reference to David.

 Read 2 Samuel 12:1-15 and **MARK** the words *poor* and *rich* and the men they refer to.

2 Samuel 12:1-15

1   Then the LORD sent Nathan to David. And he came to him and said, "There were two men in one city, the one rich and the other poor.

2   "The rich man had a great many flocks and herds.

3   "But the poor man had nothing except one little ewe lamb

    Which he bought and nourished;

    And it grew up together with him and his children.

    It would eat of his bread and drink of his cup and lie in his bosom,

    And was like a daughter to him.

4   "Now a traveler came to the rich man,

    And he was unwilling to take from his own flock or his own herd,

    To prepare for the wayfarer who had come to him;

    Rather he took the poor man's ewe lamb and prepared it for the man who had come to him."

5   Then David's anger burned greatly against the man, and he said to Nathan, "As the LORD lives, surely the man who has done this deserves to die.

6   "He must make restitution for the lamb fourfold, because he did this thing and had no compassion."

7   Nathan then said to David, "You are the man! Thus says the LORD God of Israel, 'It is I who anointed you king over Israel and it is I who delivered you from the hand of Saul.

8   'I also gave you your master's house and your master's wives into your care, and I gave you the house of Israel and Judah; and if *that had been* too little, I would have added to you many more things like these!

9   'Why have you despised the word of the LORD by doing evil in His sight? You have struck down Uriah the Hittite with the sword, have taken his wife to be your wife, and have killed him with the sword of the sons of Ammon.

10 'Now therefore, the sword shall never depart from your house, because you have despised Me and have taken the wife of Uriah the Hittite to be your wife.'

FYI:

Proverbs 22:16

He who oppresses the poor to make more for himself

Or who gives to the rich, will only come to poverty.

11 "Thus says the LORD, 'Behold, I will raise up evil against you from your own household; I will even take your wives before your eyes and give *them* to your companion, and he will lie with your wives in broad daylight.

12 'Indeed you did it secretly, but I will do this thing before all Israel, and under the sun.'"

13 Then David said to Nathan, "I have sinned against the LORD." And Nathan said to David, "The LORD also has taken away your sin; you shall not die.

14 "However, because by this deed you have given occasion to the enemies of the LORD to blaspheme, the child also that is born to you shall surely die."

15 So Nathan went to his house.

Then the LORD struck the child that Uriah's widow bore to David, so that he was *very* sick.

Discuss with your GROUP or PONDER on your own . . .

How has David changed from the man he was in 1 Samuel 18? Was he more honorable as "the poor man" or "the rich man"? Explain.

What about Nathan's story repulses David?

How does Nathan help David see his own sin? What does Nathan say about his actions?

How does David's behavior in this season differ from the description of the wise king in Proverbs 20? (See verses 8, 26, 28.)

ONE STEP FURTHER:

Riches

Take some time this week to examine what the rest of the Bible says about riches. Use a concordance to locate passages by entering key words such as "riches," "wealth," etc. Record what you observe in the Old and New Testaments. Before you finish, record warnings you notice.

Old Testament:

New Testament:

Warnings:

Savvy

GOD'S TRUTH FOR A LIFE THAT WORKS

How does David respond when his sin is exposed? What can you learn from his response to apply?

PROVERBS 21

Sorry. It's in the text and it's repeated.

Read Proverbs 21:9 and 19. **MARK** *woman* and the adjectives that describe her.

Proverbs 21:9, 19

9   It is better to live in a corner of a roof

     Than in a house shared with a contentious woman.

19   It is better to live in a desert land

     Than with a contentious and vexing woman.

Discuss with your **GROUP** or **PONDER** on your own . . .

What accommodations are better than inside with a contentious woman? What do both locations have in common? Which do you think is worse and why?

How does this woman differ from the wife of Proverbs 19:14?

Are there any circumstances in your life (whether you're a man or woman!) where you're more tempted toward contentious behavior? If so, why do you think that is?

What else does Proverbs say in 19:13 and 27:15 about contentious women?

ONE STEP FURTHER:

Want a Face?
Want a face to put with the description "vexing woman"? Check out 1 Samuel 1 and watch for the word "provoke." Record your observations below.

Savvy
GOD'S TRUTH FOR A LIFE THAT WORKS

Do you ever drip? (Sorry. Had to ask.)

What do contention and strife need to flourish? How can you identify and stop it in yourself if it starts?

ONE STEP FURTHER:

Word Study: Contentious and Vexing
If you have time this week, see what you can find out about these two "delightful" words and how they are used in Proverbs and throughout the Old Testament. Record your findings below.

Observe Proverbs 22:17–24:34

This section of the text leads with an exhortation to listen and follows with a heavy list of activities the wise forgo. Want to be wise not only in what you "do" but also in what you "don't"? Proverbs tells us how!

READ Proverbs 22:17–24:34. Just overview the chapters and enjoy the reading.

Proverbs 22

17 Incline your ear and hear the words of the wise,

And apply your mind to my knowledge;

18 For it will be pleasant if you keep them within you,

That they may be ready on your lips.

19 So that your trust may be in the LORD,

I have taught you today, even you.

20 Have I not written to you excellent things

Of counsels and knowledge,

21 To make you know the certainty of the words of truth

That you may correctly answer him who sent you?

22 Do not rob the poor because he is poor,

Or crush the afflicted at the gate;

23 For the LORD will plead their case

And take the life of those who rob them.

24 Do not associate with a man *given* to anger;

Or go with a hot-tempered man,

25 Or you will learn his ways

And find a snare for yourself.

26 Do not be among those who give pledges,

Among those who become guarantors for debts.

27 If you have nothing with which to pay,

Why should he take your bed from under you?

28 Do not move the ancient boundary

Which your fathers have set.

29 Do you see a man skilled in his work?

He will stand before kings;

He will not stand before obscure men.

Proverbs 23

1 When you sit down to dine with a ruler,

Consider carefully what is before you,

2 And put a knife to your throat

If you are a man of *great* appetite.

3 Do not desire his delicacies,

For it is deceptive food.

4 Do not weary yourself to gain wealth,

Cease from your consideration *of it.*

5 When you set your eyes on it, it is gone.

For *wealth* certainly makes itself wings

Like an eagle that flies *toward* the heavens.

6 Do not eat the bread of a selfish man,

Or desire his delicacies;

7 For as he thinks within himself, so he is.

He says to you, "Eat and drink!"

But his heart is not with you.

8 You will vomit up the morsel you have eaten,

And waste your compliments.

9 Do not speak in the hearing of a fool,

For he will despise the wisdom of your words.

10 Do not move the ancient boundary

Or go into the fields of the fatherless,

11 For their Redeemer is strong;

He will plead their case against you.

12 Apply your heart to discipline

And your ears to words of knowledge.

13 Do not hold back discipline from the child,

Although you strike him with the rod, he will not die.

14 You shall strike him with the rod

And rescue his soul from Sheol.

15 My son, if your heart is wise,

My own heart also will be glad;

16 And my inmost being will rejoice

When your lips speak what is right.

17 Do not let your heart envy sinners,

But *live* in the fear of the LORD always.

18 Surely there is a future,

And your hope will not be cut off.

19 Listen, my son, and be wise,

And direct your heart in the way.

20 Do not be with heavy drinkers of wine,

Or with gluttonous eaters of meat;

21 For the heavy drinker and the glutton will come to poverty,

And drowsiness will clothe *one* with rags.

22 Listen to your father who begot you,

And do not despise your mother when she is old.

23 Buy truth, and do not sell *it,*

Get wisdom and instruction and understanding.

24 The father of the righteous will greatly rejoice,

And he who sires a wise son will be glad in him.

25 Let your father and your mother be glad,

And let her rejoice who gave birth to you.

26 Give me your heart, my son,

And let your eyes delight in my ways.

27 For a harlot is a deep pit

And an adulterous woman is a narrow well.

28 Surely she lurks as a robber,

And increases the faithless among men.

29 Who has woe? Who has sorrow?

Who has contentions? Who has complaining?

Who has wounds without cause?

Who has redness of eyes?

30 Those who linger long over wine,

Those who go to taste mixed wine.

31 Do not look on the wine when it is red,

When it sparkles in the cup,

When it goes down smoothly;

32 At the last it bites like a serpent

And stings like a viper.

33 Your eyes will see strange things

And your mind will utter perverse things.

34 And you will be like one who lies down in the middle of the sea,

Or like one who lies down on the top of a mast.

35 "They struck me, *but* I did not become ill;

They beat me, *but* I did not know *it*.

When shall I awake?

I will seek another drink."

Proverbs 24

1 Do not be envious of evil men,
Nor desire to be with them;

2 For their minds devise violence,
And their lips talk of trouble.

3 By wisdom a house is built,

And by understanding it is established;

4 And by knowledge the rooms are filled

With all precious and pleasant riches.

5 A wise man is strong,

And a man of knowledge increases power.

6 For by wise guidance you will wage war,

And in abundance of counselors there is victory.

7 Wisdom is *too* exalted for a fool,

He does not open his mouth in the gate.

8 One who plans to do evil,
Men will call a schemer.

9 The devising of folly is sin,

And the scoffer is an abomination to men.

10 If you are slack in the day of distress,

Your strength is limited.

11 Deliver those who are being taken away to death,

And those who are staggering to slaughter, Oh *hold* them back.

12 If you say, "See, we did not know this,"

Does He not consider *it* who weighs the hearts?

And does He not know *it* who keeps your soul?

And will He not render to man according to his work?

13 My son, eat honey, for it is good,

Yes, the honey from the comb is sweet to your taste;

14 Know *that* wisdom is thus for your soul;

If you find *it,* then there will be a future,

Savvy

GOD'S TRUTH FOR A LIFE THAT WORKS

And your hope will not be cut off.

15 Do not lie in wait, O wicked man, against the dwelling of the righteous;

Do not destroy his resting place;

16 For a righteous man falls seven times, and rises again,

But the wicked stumble in *time of* calamity.

17 Do not rejoice when your enemy falls,

And do not let your heart be glad when he stumbles;

18 Or the LORD will see *it* and be displeased,

And turn His anger away from him.

19 Do not fret because of evildoers

Or be envious of the wicked;

20 For there will be no future for the evil man;

The lamp of the wicked will be put out.

21 My son, fear the LORD and the king;

Do not associate with those who are given to change,

22 For their calamity will rise suddenly,

And who knows the ruin *that comes* from both of them?

23 These also are sayings of the wise.

To show partiality in judgment is not good.

24 He who says to the wicked, "You are righteous,"

Peoples will curse him, nations will abhor him;

25 But to those who rebuke the *wicked* will be delight,

And a good blessing will come upon them.

26 He kisses the lips

Who gives a right answer.

27 Prepare your work outside

And make it ready for yourself in the field;

Afterwards, then, build your house.

28 Do not be a witness against your neighbor without cause,

And do not deceive with your lips.

29 Do not say, "Thus I shall do to him as he has done to me;

I will render to the man according to his work."

30 I passed by the field of the sluggard

And by the vineyard of the man lacking sense,

31 And behold, it was completely overgrown with thistles;

Its surface was covered with nettles,

And its stone wall was broken down.

32 When I saw, I reflected upon it;

I looked, *and* received instruction.

33 "A little sleep, a little slumber,

A little folding of the hands to rest,"

34 Then your poverty will come *as* a robber

And your want like an armed man.

Discuss with your **GROUP** or **PONDER** on your own . . .

What general observations did you make in these chapters? Be concise.

What questions do you have after reading the texts?

Read Proverbs 22:17–24:34 again. This time **MARK** key, repeated words that you notice, title each chapter, and identify the most applicable verse for you in each.

PROVERBS 22b: My Verse(s):

PROVERBS 23: My Verse(s):

PROVERBS 24: My Verse(s):

A THOUGHT FROM: *Jan*

Settling for Poverty Goes Against God's Instruction

I know people in barren circumstances who live with dignity and respect as they "make do" with meager means. Though they are poor, they are rich in spirit.

They haven't "settled" for poverty. They bring order to chaos and cleanliness to dusty rooms.

They make the most of it, whatever "it" is.

I also know people in gracious-looking circumstances who have settled for poverty of spirit. They know nothing of dignity and respect. They have embraced an attitude of entitlement, and all that is placed in their hands crumbles. Their laziness and indolent attitudes leave them barren. They know nothing of making the most of what they have. Their dust remains untouched, and the chaos around them just grows.

Being a person who makes the most of what you have, and who understands that finding many streams of income is pure brilliance, will help you do well in life. Laziness, folding the hands in satisfaction of the status quo and carelessness with what you have will bring poverty of spirit and hopelessness. The mess will remain.

Savvy
GOD'S TRUTH FOR A LIFE THAT WORKS

ONE STEP FURTHER:

Psalm 1

This week read Psalm 1 in your spare time and consider the person that *doesn't* hang out with scoffers. As you read, think about the company you keep and record your observations below.

a Closer Look

Looking back at Proverbs 22:17–24:34, list every "don't" that the writer warns against and the reason why.

Don't Do This	The Reason

Are there any items on your list that you *know* you need to deal with? Any throat-grabbers among the "don'ts"? If so, list them below and ask God to help you obey.

PROVERBS 22

Before we move on, let's look at a few of these more closely since we may have a tendency to read past things that are applicable.

READ Proverbs 22:10, 24-25. **MARK** *contention, strife, anger,* and *hot-tempered.*

Proverbs 22:10, 24-25

10 Drive out the scoffer, and contention will go out,

Even strife and dishonor will cease.

24 Do not associate with a man *given* to anger;

Or go with a hot-tempered man,

25 Or you will learn his ways

And find a snare for yourself.

Discuss with your GROUP or PONDER on your own . . .

What correlation does Proverbs 22:10 make? What kind of person hangs out with contention?

What does this say about circumstances? Put another way, if circumstances improve, will contentious behavior likely stop? Explain your answer.

Why is it important not to become entangled with scoffers and hot-tempered people?

How can you "drive out" scoffers from your head space even if you have to co-exist with them at work or at home?

Read Proverbs 22:17-21. **UNDERLINE** everything the wise do.

Proverbs 22:17-21

17   Incline your ear and hear the words of the wise,
     And apply your mind to my knowledge;

18   For it will be pleasant if you keep them within you,
     That they may be ready on your lips.

19   So that your trust may be in the LORD,
     I have taught you today, even you.

20   Have I not written to you excellent things
     Of counsels and knowledge,

21   To make you know the certainty of the words of truth
     That you may correctly answer him who sent you?

Savvy
GOD'S TRUTH FOR A LIFE THAT WORKS

Discuss with your GROUP or PONDER on your own . . .

What will the wise reader do based on these verses? Why?

How are you doing with this practically, day by day?

Read Proverbs 22:22-23 and **MARK** every reference to *the poor*, including pronouns.

Proverbs 22:22-23

22   Do not rob the poor because he is poor,

Or crush the afflicted at the gate;

23   For the LORD will plead their case

And take the life of those who rob them.

Discuss with your GROUP or PONDER on your own . . .

What does the text say about how the wise will treat the poor? Why will they do this?

What came to your mind when you first read this?

Are there other ways the poor can be robbed or afflicted today?

Have you ever found yourself on the receiving end of crushed, afflicted, or robbed? If so, how can this help you sympathize with the plight of others and help them?

Did you notice other proverbs in this section that relate to this? If so, which ones and how are they related?

In the end, who will those who treat the poor badly have to answer to? How should this impact their behavior?

Sometimes lack is a result of oppression, but that is not always the case. Sometimes lack is a result of our own sloth. Let's take a look.

Read Proverbs 24:30-34 and **MARK** every reference to *the field of the sluggard,* including pronouns.

Proverbs 24:30-34

30   I passed by the field of the sluggard
       And by the vineyard of the man lacking sense,

31   And behold, it was completely overgrown with thistles;
       Its surface was covered with nettles,
       And its stone wall was broken down.

32   When I saw, I reflected upon it;
       I looked, *and* received instruction.

33   "A little sleep, a little slumber,
       A little folding of the hands to rest,"

34   Then your poverty will come *as* a robber
       And your want like an armed man.

Discuss with your GROUP or PONDER on your own . . .

What possessions does the sluggard have? What condition are they in?

Savvy
GOD'S TRUTH FOR A LIFE THAT WORKS

How does this man treat the possessions he has? What is the result?

Why did poverty come on him? How does he differ from the poor man of Proverbs 22?

When acquiring new things, do you ever consider how you've maintained what you already have and whether you can maintain more?

What lesson are we to draw from this? What are you applying?

@THE END OF THE DAY . . .

Take some time to summarize what you've learned this week and over the past few weeks. What proverbs are most changing the way you think and act? Once you've thought through this broadly, think back more specifically. What one proverb or category of proverbs do you need to pay more attention to moving forward? Ask God to help you see any pockets of foolishness in your life. Then accept and act on the correction you see in His Word. Jot down anything you need to remember.

Solomon, Agur, and Lemuel

Charm is deceitful and beauty is vain,
But a woman who fears the LORD, she shall be praised.
–Proverbs 31:30

The final chapters of Proverbs offer words from Solomon and two other men named Agur and Lemuel who note the wonder of God, the blessings of wisdom, and the gift of a woman who fears the LORD.

As you study this week, ask God to help you continue to grow in wisdom when our study is complete.

ONE STEP FURTHER:

Hezekiah, King of Judah

Take some time this week to get to know King Hezekiah! Use a concordance to locate specific passages about him in the Bible and then read the accounts of his life and rule to see what you can discover about him. As with other kings you've studied, you'll find out about him primarily in the Kings and Chronicles, but he also shows up prominently in one of the major prophets! Record what you discover below, and note both wise and foolish incidents in his life.

Observe Proverbs 25-29: Proverbs of Solomon

Again we see Proverbs attributed to Solomon, this time by way of Hezekiah's men.

READ and enjoy Proverbs 25-29. Questions follow on page 138.

Proverbs 25

1 These also are proverbs of Solomon which the men of Hezekiah, king of Judah, transcribed.

2 It is the glory of God to conceal a matter,
But the glory of kings is to search out a matter.

3 *As* the heavens for height and the earth for depth,
So the heart of kings is unsearchable.

4 Take away the dross from the silver,
And there comes out a vessel for the smith;

5 Take away the wicked before the king,
And his throne will be established in righteousness.

6 Do not claim honor in the presence of the king,
And do not stand in the place of great men;

7 For it is better that it be said to you, "Come up here,"
Than for you to be placed lower in the presence of the prince,
Whom your eyes have seen.

8 Do not go out hastily to argue *your case;*
Otherwise, what will you do in the end,
When your neighbor humiliates you?

9 Argue your case with your neighbor,
And do not reveal the secret of another,

10 Or he who hears *it* will reproach you,
And the evil report about you will not pass away.

11 *Like* apples of gold in settings of silver
Is a word spoken in right circumstances.

12 *Like* an earring of gold and an ornament of fine gold
Is a wise reprover to a listening ear.

13 Like the cold of snow in the time of harvest
Is a faithful messenger to those who send him,
For he refreshes the soul of his masters.

14 *Like* clouds and wind without rain
Is a man who boasts of his gifts falsely.

15 By forbearance a ruler may be persuaded,
And a soft tongue breaks the bone.

16 Have you found honey?
Eat *only* what you need,
That you not have it in excess and vomit it.

17 Let your foot rarely be in your neighbor's house,
Or he will become weary of you and hate you.

18 *Like* a club and a sword and a sharp arrow
Is a man who bears false witness against his neighbor.

19 *Like* a bad tooth and an unsteady foot
Is confidence in a faithless man in time of trouble.

GOD'S TRUTH FOR A LIFE THAT WORKS

20 *Like* one who takes off a garment on a cold day, or *like* vinegar on soda,

Is he who sings songs to a troubled heart.

21 If your enemy is hungry, give him food to eat;

And if he is thirsty, give him water to drink;

22 For you will heap burning coals on his head,

And the LORD will reward you.

23 The north wind brings forth rain,

And a backbiting tongue, an angry countenance.

24 It is better to live in a corner of the roof

Than in a house shared with a contentious woman.

25 *Like* cold water to a weary soul,

So is good news from a distant land.

26 *Like* a trampled spring and a polluted well

Is a righteous man who gives way before the wicked.

27 It is not good to eat much honey,

Nor is it glory to search out one's own glory.

28 *Like* a city that is broken into *and* without walls

Is a man who has no control over his spirit.

Proverbs 26

1 Like snow in summer and like rain in harvest,

So honor is not fitting for a fool.

2 Like a sparrow in *its* flitting, like a swallow in *its* flying,

So a curse without cause does not alight.

3 A whip is for the horse, a bridle for the donkey,

And a rod for the back of fools.

4 Do not answer a fool according to his folly,

Or you will also be like him.

5 Answer a fool as his folly *deserves,*

That he not be wise in his own eyes.

6 He cuts off *his own* feet *and* drinks violence

Who sends a message by the hand of a fool.

7 *Like* the legs *which* are useless to the lame,

So is a proverb in the mouth of fools.

8 Like one who binds a stone in a sling,

So is he who gives honor to a fool.

9 *Like* a thorn *which* falls into the hand of a drunkard,

So is a proverb in the mouth of fools.

10 *Like* an archer who wounds everyone,

So is he who hires a fool or who hires those who pass by.

11 Like a dog that returns to its vomit

Is a fool who repeats his folly.

12 Do you see a man wise in his own eyes?

There is more hope for a fool than for him.

13 The sluggard says, "There is a lion in the road!

A lion is in the open square!"

14 *As* the door turns on its hinges,

So *does* the sluggard on his bed.

15 The sluggard buries his hand in the dish;

He is weary of bringing it to his mouth again.

16 The sluggard is wiser in his own eyes

Than seven men who can give a discreet answer.

17 *Like* one who takes a dog by the ears

Savvy

GOD'S TRUTH FOR A LIFE THAT WORKS

133

Is he who passes by *and* meddles with strife not belonging to him.

18 Like a madman who throws
Firebrands, arrows and death,

19 So is the man who deceives his neighbor,
And says, "Was I not joking?"

20 For lack of wood the fire goes out,
And where there is no whisperer, contention quiets down.

21 *Like* charcoal to hot embers and wood to fire,
So is a contentious man to kindle strife.

22 The words of a whisperer are like dainty morsels,
And they go down into the innermost parts of the body.

23 *Like* an earthen vessel overlaid with silver dross

Are burning lips and a wicked heart.

24 He who hates disguises *it* with his lips,
But he lays up deceit in his heart.

25 When he speaks graciously, do not believe him,
For there are seven abominations in his heart.

26 *Though his* hatred covers itself with guile,
His wickedness will be revealed before the assembly.

27 He who digs a pit will fall into it,
And he who rolls a stone, it will come back on him.

28 A lying tongue hates those it crushes,
And a flattering mouth works ruin.

Proverbs 27

1 Do not boast about tomorrow,
For you do not know what a day may bring forth.

2 Let another praise you, and not your own mouth;
A stranger, and not your own lips.

3 A stone is heavy and the sand weighty,
But the provocation of a fool is heavier than both of them.

4 Wrath is fierce and anger is a flood,
But who can stand before jealousy?

5 Better is open rebuke
Than love that is concealed.

6 Faithful are the wounds of a friend,
But deceitful are the kisses of an enemy.

7 A sated man loathes honey,
But to a famished man any bitter thing is sweet.

8 Like a bird that wanders from her nest,
So is a man who wanders from his home.

9 Oil and perfume make the heart glad,
So a man's counsel is sweet to his friend.

10 Do not forsake your own friend or your father's friend,
And do not go to your brother's house in the day of your calamity;
Better is a neighbor who is near than a brother far away.

11 Be wise, my son, and make my heart glad,
That I may reply to him who reproaches me.

12 A prudent man sees evil *and* hides himself,
The naive proceed *and* pay the penalty.

13 Take his garment when he becomes surety for a stranger;

GOD'S TRUTH FOR A LIFE THAT WORKS

134

And for an adulterous woman hold him in pledge.

14 He who blesses his friend with a loud voice early in the morning,

It will be reckoned a curse to him.

15 A constant dripping on a day of steady rain

And a contentious woman are alike;

16 He who would restrain her restrains the wind,

And grasps oil with his right hand.

17 Iron sharpens iron,

So one man sharpens another.

18 He who tends the fig tree will eat its fruit,

And he who cares for his master will be honored.

19 As in water face *reflects* face,

So the heart of man *reflects* man.

20 Sheol and Abaddon are never satisfied,

Nor are the eyes of man ever satisfied.

21 The crucible is for silver and the furnace for gold,

And each *is tested* by the praise accorded him.

22 Though you pound a fool in a mortar with a pestle along with crushed grain,

Yet his foolishness will not depart from him.

23 Know well the condition of your flocks,

And pay attention to your herds;

24 For riches are not forever,

Nor does a crown *endure* to all generations.

25 *When* the grass disappears, the new growth is seen,

And the herbs of the mountains are gathered in,

26 The lambs *will be* for your clothing,

And the goats *will bring* the price of a field,

27 And *there will be* goats' milk enough for your food,

For the food of your household,

And sustenance for your maidens.

Proverbs 28

1 The wicked flee when no one is pursuing,

But the righteous are bold as a lion.

2 By the transgression of a land many are its princes,

But by a man of understanding *and* knowledge, so it endures.

3 A poor man who oppresses the lowly

Is *like* a driving rain which leaves no food.

4 Those who forsake the law praise the wicked,

But those who keep the law strive with them.

5 Evil men do not understand justice,

But those who seek the LORD understand all things.

6 Better is the poor who walks in his integrity

Than he who is crooked though he be rich.

7 He who keeps the law is a discerning son,

But he who is a companion of gluttons humiliates his father.

8 He who increases his wealth by interest and usury

Gathers it for him who is gracious to the poor.

9 He who turns away his ear from listening to the law,

Even his prayer is an abomination.

10 He who leads the upright astray in an evil way

Will himself fall into his own pit,

Savvy

GOD'S TRUTH FOR A LIFE THAT WORKS

But the blameless will inherit good.

11 The rich man is wise in his own eyes,

But the poor who has understanding sees through him.

12 When the righteous triumph, there is great glory,

But when the wicked rise, men hide themselves.

13 He who conceals his transgressions will not prosper,

But he who confesses and forsakes *them* will find compassion.

14 How blessed is the man who fears always,

But he who hardens his heart will fall into calamity.

15 *Like* a roaring lion and a rushing bear

Is a wicked ruler over a poor people.

16 A leader who is a great oppressor lacks understanding,

But he who hates unjust gain will prolong *his* days.

17 A man who is laden with the guilt of human blood

Will be a fugitive until death; let no one support him.

18 He who walks blamelessly will be delivered,

But he who is crooked will fall all at once.

19 He who tills his land will have plenty of food,

But he who follows empty *pursuits* will have poverty in plenty.

20 A faithful man will abound with blessings,

But he who makes haste to be rich will not go unpunished.

21 To show partiality is not good,

Because for a piece of bread a man will transgress.

22 A man with an evil eye hastens after wealth

And does not know that want will come upon him.

23 He who rebukes a man will afterward find *more* favor

Than he who flatters with the tongue.

24 He who robs his father or his mother

And says, "It is not a transgression,"

Is the companion of a man who destroys.

25 An arrogant man stirs up strife,

But he who trusts in the LORD will prosper.

26 He who trusts in his own heart is a fool,

But he who walks wisely will be delivered.

27 He who gives to the poor will never want,

But he who shuts his eyes will have many curses.

28 When the wicked rise, men hide themselves;

But when they perish, the righteous increase.

Proverbs 29

1 A man who hardens *his* neck after much reproof

Will suddenly be broken beyond remedy.

2 When the righteous increase, the people rejoice,

But when a wicked man rules, people groan.

3 A man who loves wisdom makes his father glad,

But he who keeps company with harlots wastes *his* wealth.

4 The king gives stability to the land by justice,

But a man who takes bribes overthrows it.

5 A man who flatters his neighbor
Is spreading a net for his steps.

6 By transgression an evil man is ensnared,

But the righteous sings and rejoices.

7 The righteous is concerned for the rights of the poor,

The wicked does not understand *such* concern.

8 Scorners set a city aflame,

But wise men turn away anger.

9 When a wise man has a controversy with a foolish man,

The foolish man either rages or laughs, and there is no rest.

10 Men of bloodshed hate the blameless,

But the upright are concerned for his life.

11 A fool always loses his temper,

But a wise man holds it back.

12 If a ruler pays attention to falsehood,

All his ministers *become* wicked.

13 The poor man and the oppressor have this in common:

The LORD gives light to the eyes of both.

14 If a king judges the poor with truth,

His throne will be established forever.

15 The rod and reproof give wisdom,

But a child who gets his own way brings shame to his mother.

16 When the wicked increase, transgression increases;

But the righteous will see their fall.

17 Correct your son, and he will give you comfort;

He will also delight your soul.

18 Where there is no vision, the people are unrestrained,

But happy is he who keeps the law.

19 A slave will not be instructed by words *alone;*

For though he understands, there will be no response.

20 Do you see a man who is hasty in his words?

There is more hope for a fool than for him.

21 He who pampers his slave from childhood

Will in the end find him to be a son.

22 An angry man stirs up strife,

And a hot-tempered man abounds in transgression.

23 A man's pride will bring him low,

But a humble spirit will obtain honor.

24 He who is a partner with a thief hates his own life;

He hears the oath but tells nothing.

25 The fear of man brings a snare,

But he who trusts in the LORD will be exalted.

26 Many seek the ruler's favor,

But justice for man *comes* from the LORD.

27 An unjust man is abominable to the righteous,

And he who is upright in the way is abominable to the wicked.

Discuss with your GROUP or PONDER on your own . . .

What general observations did you make in these chapters? Be concise.

What questions do you have after reading the text?

Read Proverbs 25–29 again. This time **MARK** key, repeated words that you notice, title each chapter, and identify the most applicable verse for you in each.

PROVERBS 25: My Verse(s):

PROVERBS 26: My Verse(s):

PROVERBS 27: My Verse(s):

PROVERBS 28: My Verse(s):

A THOUGHT FROM: *Pam*

Where's the address?

By now you may be asking yourself, "Why doesn't she tell me where to find the references? Why do I have to figure out some of my own cross-references?"

The answer to this question is simple: so you will be equipped to do it for yourself. When I was growing up, my mom always did my laundry. I had no reason to learn to do it since someone else always took care of it. There was no compelling reason to learn. When I got married and moved out, I started doing it myself. The need to have clean clothes compelled me to learn.

It wasn't hard, but until then I had no reason to try. Same thing with Scripture references. It's not hard to find them with the tools we have available today, but if someone's always doing it for you, why bother?

That is why you get to find some of your own references. I want you equipped to know truth for yourself, not dependent on me to show you where to find it.

Savvy

GOD'S TRUTH FOR A LIFE THAT WORKS

PROVERBS 29: My Verse(s):

PROVERBS 25
Discuss with your GROUP or PONDER on your own . . .

Looking back at 25:1-15, what principles do these proverbs teach about kings, princes, rulers and how to live with them?

Based on these verses, what are some effective ways to influence leaders? How do these compare with the ways your culture operates?

Did you notice the simile parade that starts in Proverbs 25:11 and marches through Proverbs 26? Go ahead and mark them in the text with a simple underline. Then pick five that you find most applicable to your life today and record them below.

Like	So Is/Are	Why/Lesson

Did the similes you picked have common themes? If so, what were they?

A THOUGHT FROM: *Pam*

Reading Past . . .
So many people today disregard the pure Word of God as "too general" in favor of wise people on the top of best seller lists who speak pointed words to specific cultural situations. I'm guessing these folks haven't read the book of Proverbs recently. When we slow down and take them seriously, we realize they are too specific to escape and far too practical to ignore.

FYI:

Grade School English
In case you're a few years removed from school, a simile is a figure of speech that compares two things to help the reader see comparisons (likenesses) that are not evident. This is why the comparison uses "like" or "as" as in "busy like a bee."

Similes in Proverbs paint vivid pictures that help me remember not to do things like poke my nose into someone else's argument. It doesn't seem that dangerous on the front end, but anyone who's ever done it knows that you're as likely to get bit as a person grabbing a dog's ears! Similes work for me!

Savvy
GOD'S TRUTH FOR A LIFE THAT WORKS

What life situation prompted you to pick these similes? How will you apply them? (You can address all five or pick the one most significant to you. Remember we're on a long journey in the same direction. Better to pick one and focus than to pick five and forget.)

ONE STEP FURTHER:

Neighbors

Have you noticed all the references to neighbors in Proverbs? Summarize what you've learned about neighbors that is changing the way you think and act. As you do, remember to read Luke 10:25-37 to see how Jesus defines "neighbor." Record what you've learned below.

a Closer Look

PROVERBS 26

Let's spend a little more time with the mouth. (Can you tell where God is working on me?!)

READ Proverbs 26:17-21 and **MARK** references to people who behave foolishly, including pronouns.

Proverbs 26:17-21

17   *Like* one who takes a dog by the ears

Is he who passes by *and* meddles with strife not belonging to him.

18   Like a madman who throws

Firebrands, arrows and death,

19   So is the man who deceives his neighbor,

And says, "Was I not joking?"

20   For lack of wood the fire goes out,

And where there is no whisperer, contention quiets down.

21   *Like* charcoal to hot embers and wood to fire,

So is a contentious man to kindle strife.

Discuss with your GROUP or PONDER on your own . . .

What foolish behavior does Solomon describe in these verses? What commonalities did you notice?

What should your posture be toward strife that is not yours? Put another way, if you don't have a dog in the fight, what should you do? According to this proverb, why is this?

Savvy

GOD'S TRUTH FOR A LIFE THAT WORKS

Have you figuratively "grabbed a dog by the ears"? How has it gone? What have you learned?

What verbal abuses do the remaining verses address?

If you are not typically a "whisperer," how can you help prevent the whispering of others?

What situations tempt you to "whisper"? Are you typically aware when you're doing it or do you realize it after the fact? How can you engage others to help you put out the fire?

PROVERBS 27

Proverbs 27 talks at some length about friendship, which we'll look at shortly. First, though, let's check out what it says about a common problem in our culture: boasting. It's something we like to polish up to look like humility, but bragging is bragging regardless of how it's dressed.

Read Proverbs 27:1-4 and **MARK** all *mouth/lips* references.

Proverbs 27:1-4

1   Do not boast about tomorrow,

    For you do not know what a day may bring forth.

2   Let another praise you, and not your own mouth;

    A stranger, and not your own lips.

3   A stone is heavy and the sand weighty,

    But the provocation of a fool is heavier than both of them.

4   Wrath is fierce and anger is a flood,

    But who can stand before jealousy?

The One Thing to Boast

Thus says the LORD, "Let not a wise man boast of his wisdom, and let not the mighty man boast of his might, let not a rich man boast of his riches; but let him who boasts boast of this, that he understands and knows Me, that I am the LORD who exercises lovingkindness, justice and righteousness on earth; for I delight in these things," declares the LORD.

—Jeremiah 9:23-24

Savvy

GOD'S TRUTH FOR A LIFE THAT WORKS

A THOUGHT FROM: *Jan*

Faithful Wounds, Deceitful Kisses

The gift of friendship is the gift of being faithful in all things. A friend can be trusted to have your back. When someone has targeted you for a gossipy comment, a friend will cover your back. When someone is coming in from the side with a subtle manipulation, a friend will see it and cover your flank. If you make a fool of yourself, a friend won't deny she knows you and will just "throw a tent over it." She won't become one of your critics, but if you need the gentle encouragement to repent and walk another path or to avoid a foolish situation or to return to your roots, she'll be there to call you back. That's what friends are for. Sometimes her words will wound your sense of being "all that", but those are the wounds that do a healing work. They come from a faithful love.

There are those who will flatter to please you. They will shower compliments on you when there is nothing to compliment and you know it. They don't have your back nor do they cover your side. They just want "something." They are not seeking your highest good. They are using you and your good graces for their own good. Hopefully, there is no one like that in your life but, if there is, you can know they will "kiss" you with a "deceitful kiss" and then they'll move on. There is no faithfulness in their "love." Their relationship is no gift. It is an arrangement that can be too much to bear.

Knowing the difference between a friend and an enemy is a relational skill. Proverbs is full of relational instruction. Absorb it well. Before this life is over, you will probably need it.

Discuss with your GROUP or PONDER on your own . . .

What mouth sin does this section warn against? How do you see this exhibited in culture today? What industries are built on it?

How does it show itself in everyday life? In *your* life?

When you run into bragging ("humble" brag or otherwise) in others, does it trigger anything in you? If so, what?

Do you think bragging provokes jealousy? Explain.

How can you guard your heart against both sides of this sharp sword?

Read Proverbs 27:6 and 17 and **MARK** all references to people.

Proverbs 27:6, 17

6   Faithful are the wounds of a friend,
    But deceitful are the kisses of an enemy.

17   Iron sharpens iron,
     So one man sharpens another.

Discuss with your GROUP or PONDER on your own . . .

What people do these verses talk about?

What surprising actions are attributed to friends and enemies in verse 6? Have you ever had a faithful wound? Briefly describe the situation and how you were benefited. How did it feel in the moment?

What about a deceitful kiss? Have you ever given one, received one, or witnessed one? How did that feel short-term? Long-term?

What are strong men compared to in verse 17? What is the benefit, and where does it come from?

Are you a friend who sharpens others? If so, how?

Briefly describe a person in your life who has had a sharpening effect on you.

Savvy
GOD'S TRUTH FOR A LIFE THAT WORKS

PROVERBS 28-29

Read back through Proverbs 28 and 29 paying close attention to the two types of people mentioned and the two paths they walk. **UNDERLINE** in one color every person who is a positive example. **UNDERLINE** in another color every negative example.

Discuss with your GROUP or PONDER on your own . . .

How are the wicked's words and actions described?

Do you see overlap or connections in the actions and attitudes attributed to the wicked? If so, what?

How does our culture define good and evil, righteous and wicked? How does this differ from what God says in His Word?

Take some time to list a few behaviors our culture says are "just fine" that Proverbs says are wrong. What do you do with this?

Now, go back and survey how the words and actions of the righteous are described.

What benefits will the righteous have? How do the righteous benefit others?

What truth from these Proverbs do you most need to hold onto and why?

Observe Proverbs 30: The Proverbs of Agur

READ Proverbs 30 paying close attention to the patterns and word pictures.

Proverbs 30

1 The words of Agur the son of Jakeh, the oracle.

The man declares to Ithiel, to Ithiel and Ucal:

2 Surely I am more stupid than any man,

And I do not have the understanding of a man.

3 Neither have I learned wisdom,

Nor do I have the knowledge of the Holy One.

4 Who has ascended into heaven and descended?

Who has gathered the wind in His fists?

Who has wrapped the waters in His garment?

Who has established all the ends of the earth?

What is His name or His son's name?

Surely you know!

5 Every word of God is tested;

He is a shield to those who take refuge in Him.

6 Do not add to His words

Or He will reprove you, and you will be proved a liar.

7 Two things I asked of You,

Do not refuse me before I die:

8 Keep deception and lies far from me,

Give me neither poverty nor riches;

Feed me with the food that is my portion,

9 That I not be full and deny *You* and say, "Who is the LORD?"

Or that I not be in want and steal,

And profane the name of my God.

10 Do not slander a slave to his master,

Or he will curse you and you will be found guilty.

11 There is a kind of *man* who curses his father

And does not bless his mother.

12 There is a kind who is pure in his own eyes,

Yet is not washed from his filthiness.

13 There is a kind—oh how lofty are his eyes!

And his eyelids are raised *in arrogance.*

14 There is a kind of *man* whose teeth are *like* swords

And his jaw teeth *like* knives,

To devour the afflicted from the earth

And the needy from among men.

15 The leech has two daughters, "Give," "Give."

There are three things that will not be satisfied,

Four that will not say, "Enough":

16 Sheol, and the barren womb,

Earth that is never satisfied with water,

And fire that never says, "Enough."

17 The eye that mocks a father

And scorns a mother,

The ravens of the valley will pick it out,

And the young eagles will eat it.

18 There are three things which are too wonderful for me,

Four which I do not understand:

19 The way of an eagle in the sky,

The way of a serpent on a rock,

The way of a ship in the middle of the sea,

And the way of a man with a maid.

20 This is the way of an adulterous woman:

She eats and wipes her mouth,

And says, "I have done no wrong."

21 Under three things the earth quakes,

And under four, it cannot bear up:

22 Under a slave when he becomes king,

And a fool when he is satisfied with food,

23 Under an unloved woman when she gets a husband,

And a maidservant when she supplants her mistress.

24 Four things are small on the earth,

But they are exceedingly wise:

25 The ants are not a strong people,

But they prepare their food in the summer;

26 The shephanim are not mighty people,

Yet they make their houses in the rocks;

27 The locusts have no king,

Yet all of them go out in ranks;

28 The lizard you may grasp with the hands,

Yet it is in kings' palaces.

29 There are three things which are stately in *their* march,

Even four which are stately when they walk:

30 The lion *which* is mighty among beasts

And does not retreat before any,

31 The strutting rooster, the male goat also,

And a king *when his* army is with him.

32 If you have been foolish in exalting yourself

Or if you have plotted *evil, put your* hand on your mouth.

33 For the churning of milk produces butter,

And pressing the nose brings forth blood;

So the churning of anger produces strife.

Savvy
GOD'S TRUTH FOR A LIFE THAT WORKS

Discuss with your GROUP or PONDER on your own . . .

Who are the words of Proverbs 30 attributed to? What do we know about him?

How does the author describe himself and his knowledge?

What do we learn about his view of God and His Word?

What does he ask God for?

What patterns did you notice in the text? What observations has Agur made about life?

FYI:

Evil Good; Good Evil

Woe to those who call evil good, and good evil; who substitute darkness for light and light for darkness; who substitute bitter for sweet and sweet for bitter! Woe to those who are wise in their own eyes and clever in their own sight!

—Isaiah 5:20-21

a Closer Look

PROVERBS 30

Before we move on, let's look closer at one verse from this section.

READ Proverbs 30:20 and **MARK** references to the *adulterous woman* including pronouns.

Proverbs 30:20

20   This is the way of an adulterous woman:

      She eats and wipes her mouth,

      And says, "I have done no wrong."

Discuss with your GROUP or PONDER on your own . . .

How does the adulterous woman behave according to Proverbs 30:20? Is any aspect of her behavior more off-putting to you than other aspects? If so, what and why?

Read Isaiah 5:20-21 and compare with Proverbs 30:20. What happens to those who contradict God's definitions of good and evil?

What have you learned so far in Proverbs that can help you stand firm in a culture that calls evil good and good evil?

Observe Proverbs 31: The Proverbs of Lemuel

Our Proverbs journey started with a father's words and ends with a mother's counsel. Read the final chapter of Proverbs and answer the questions that follow.

Proverbs 31

1 The words of King Lemuel, the oracle which his mother taught him:

2 What, O my son?

And what, O son of my womb?

And what, O son of my vows?

3 Do not give your strength to women,

Or your ways to that which destroys kings.

4 It is not for kings, O Lemuel,

It is not for kings to drink wine,

Or for rulers to desire strong drink,

5 For they will drink and forget what is decreed,

And pervert the rights of all the afflicted.

6 Give strong drink to him who is perishing,

And wine to him whose life is bitter.

7 Let him drink and forget his poverty

And remember his trouble no more.

8 Open your mouth for the mute,

For the rights of all the unfortunate.

9 Open your mouth, judge righteously,

And defend the rights of the afflicted and needy.

10 An excellent wife, who can find?

For her worth is far above jewels.

11 The heart of her husband trusts in her,

And he will have no lack of gain.

12 She does him good and not evil

All the days of her life.

13 She looks for wool and flax

And works with her hands in delight.

14 She is like merchant ships;

She brings her food from afar.

15 She rises also while it is still night

And gives food to her household

And portions to her maidens.

16 She considers a field and buys it;

From her earnings she plants a vineyard.

17 She girds herself with strength

And makes her arms strong.

18 She senses that her gain is good;

Her lamp does not go out at night.

19 She stretches out her hands to the distaff,

And her hands grasp the spindle.

20 She extends her hand to the poor,

And she stretches out her hands to the needy.

21 She is not afraid of the snow for her household,

For all her household are clothed with scarlet.

22 She makes coverings for herself;

Her clothing is fine linen and purple.

23 Her husband is known in the gates,

When he sits among the elders of the land.

Savvy

GOD'S TRUTH FOR A LIFE THAT WORKS

24 She makes linen garments and sells *them,*
And supplies belts to the tradesmen.

25 Strength and dignity are her clothing,
And she smiles at the future.

26 She opens her mouth in wisdom,
And the teaching of kindness is on her tongue.

27 She looks well to the ways of her household,
And does not eat the bread of idleness.

28 Her children rise up and bless her;
Her husband *also,* and he praises her, *saying:*

29 "Many daughters have done nobly,
But you excel them all."

30 Charm is deceitful and beauty is vain,
But a woman who fears the LORD, she shall be praised.

31 Give her the product of her hands,
And let her works praise her in the gates.

Discuss with your GROUP or PONDER on your own . . .

What warnings fill verses 1-9? Why specific warnings are given? What dangers does each situation present? What exhortations are joined to the warnings?

According to this text, what "ways" have potential to destroy kings?

What dangers does strong drink pose? What is its benefit?

How is the king to behave by contrast?

How do the women of Proverbs 31:3 compare with the excellent wife?

Describe the excellent wife. What is her value? Why?

How does she treat those around her?

How does she contribute to her household?

How are her arms described? How does she use them? What about her hands?

Does anything shake her or ruffle her feathers? Why/why not?

Remember the Power Source!

As we come to the end of our time in Proverbs, I'm reminded of all the eyes I've looked into over the years when the topic of Proverbs 31 comes up. How could any woman ever measure up to Proverbs 31's woman? While she inspires some, she overwhelms most—myself included in the latter group.

It's so easy to imagine her today having the perfect life, the perfect house, and nary a Pinterest fail! When we view her by her actions alone, though, we miss the core of what makes her excellent!

The Proverbs 31 woman will be praised because she fears the LORD!

As I consider her, I'm reminded that as I seek to follow God's ways and live out the wisdom that He has revealed in His Word—in Proverbs and everywhere else in Scripture—the power is not in me. While Proverbs tells us what kinds of behaviors work in life, it is the indwelling Holy Spirit who empowers a life that consistently lives a life of wisdom!

How is her mouth described? How does this compare with what we've seen throughout Proverbs?

What does she *not* do?

What is at her core? What makes her who she is? How does this compare with what we learned in the opening chapters of Proverbs?

What about her encourages you? Challenges you?

@THE END OF THE DAY . . .

As we finish this study, my prayer for us comes from Proverbs 1 and 2 Chronicles 16:9. Lord, as we walk through life, let us hear and increase in learning, cause us to seek and acquire wise counsel, and help us to fear You and follow You with whole hearts!

What are your next steps? How will you apply the wisdom that you've gained? What will you do to keep increasing in wisdom?

RESOURCES

Helpful Study Tools

How to Study Your Bible
Eugene, Oregon: Harvest House
Publishers

The New Inductive Study Bible
Eugene, Oregon: Harvest House
Publishers

Logos Bible Software
Available at www.logos.com.

Greek Word Study Tools

Kittel, G.; Friedrich, G.; & Bromiley,
G.W.
*Theological Dictionary of the New
Testament, Abridged* (also known as
Little Kittel)
Grand Rapids, Michigan: W.B.
Eerdmans Publishing Company

Zodhiates, Spiros
*The Complete Word Study Dictionary:
New Testament*
Chattanooga, Tennessee: AMG
Publishers

Hebrew Word Study Tools

Harris, R.L.; Archer, G.L.; & Waltke,
B.K.
*Theological Wordbook of the Old
Testament* (also known as TWOT)
Chicago, Illinois: Moody Press

Baker, Warren, and Eugene E.
Carpenter.
*The Complete Word Study Dictionary:
Old Testament*
Chattanooga, Tennessee: AMG
Publishers

General Word Study Tools

Strong, James
*The New Strong's Exhaustive
Concordance of the Bible*
Nashville, Tennessee: Thomas Nelson

Recommended Commentary Sets

Expositor's Bible Commentary
Grand Rapids, Michigan: Zondervan

NIV Application Commentary
Grand Rapids, Michigan: Zondervan

The New American Commentary
Nashville, Tennessee: Broadman and
Holman Publishers

One-Volume Commentaries

Carson, D.A.; France, R.T.; Motyer,
J.A.; & Wenham, G.J., Eds.
*New Bible Commentary: 21st Century
Edition*
Downers Grove, Illinois: InterVarsity
Press

Rydelnik, M.; Vanlaningham, M., Eds.
The Moody Bible Commentary
Chicago, Illinois: Moody Publishers

HOW TO DO AN ONLINE WORD STUDY

For use with www.blueletterbible.org

1. Type in Bible verse. Change the version to NASB. Click the "Search" button.

2. When you arrive at the next screen, you will see a "Tools" button to left of your verse. Hover your mouse over the "Tools" button and select "Interlinear" (C) to bring up concordance information.

3. Click on the Strong's number which is the link to the original word in Greek or Hebrew.

Clicking this number will bring up another screen that will give you a brief definition of the word as well as list every occurrence of the Greek word in the New Testament or Hebrew word in the Old Testament. Before running to the dictionary definition, scan places where this word is used in Scripture and examine the general contexts where it is used.

ABOUT PRECEPT

Precept Ministries International was raised up by God for the sole purpose of establishing people in God's Word to produce reverence for Him. It serves as an arm of the church without respect to denomination. God has enabled Precept to reach across denominational lines without compromising the truths of His inerrant Word. We believe every word of the Bible was inspired and given to man as all that is necessary for him to become mature and thoroughly equipped for every good work of life. This ministry does not seek to impose its doctrines on others, but rather to direct people to the Master Himself, who leads and guides by His Spirit into all truth through a systematic study of His Word. The ministry produces a variety of Bible studies and holds conferences and intensive Training Workshops designed to establish attendees in the Word through Inductive Bible Study.

Jack Arthur and his wife, Kay, founded Precept Ministries in 1970. Kay and the ministry staff of writers produce **Precept Upon Precept**® studies, **In & Out**® studies, **Lord** series studies, the **New Inductive Study Series** studies, **40-Minute** studies, and **Discover 4 Yourself**® **Inductive Bible Studies for Kids**. From years of diligent study and teaching experience, Kay and the staff have developed these unique, inductive courses that are now used in nearly 180 countries and 70 languages.

PRECEPT.ORG

PAM GILLASPIE

Pam Gillaspie, a passionate Bible student and teacher, authors Precept's *Sweeter Than Chocolate!*® and *Cookies on the Lower Shelf*™ Bible study series. Pam holds a BA in Biblical Studies from Wheaton College in Wheaton, Illinois. She and her husband live in suburban Chicago, Illinois, with their daughter and Great Dane. They also have a married son and a new daughter-in-love. Pam's greatest joy is encouraging others to read God's Word widely and study it deeply . . . precept upon precept.

Connect with Pam at:

www.pamgillaspie.com

 pamgillaspie

 pamgillaspie

JAN SILVIOUS

Jan Silvious, an author, speaker, and professional life coach, is known for her biblically sound, psychologically positive answers to women's challenges. A former radio co-host with Kay Arthur for five years, Jan was also a speaker for eight years with Women of Faith®. She and her husband have three sons, two daughters-in-law, and five grandchildren and live in Chattanooga, Tennessee.

www.jansilvious.com

 jansilvious

 jansilvious

CPSIA information can be obtained
at www.ICGtesting.com
Printed in the USA
LVHW01s0347040118
561593LV00003B/3/P